The Nice Valour by Thomas Middleton & John Fletcher

Or, The Passionate Madman

Previously attributed to Fletcher & Beaumont

Thomas Middleton was born in London in April 1580 and baptised on 18th April.

Middleton was aged only five when his father died. His mother remarried but this unfortunately fell apart into a fifteen year legal dispute regarding the inheritance due Thomas and his younger sister.

By the time he left Oxford, at the turn of the Century, Middleton had and published Microcynicon: Six Snarling Satirese which was denounced by the Archbishop of Canterbury and publicly burned.

In the early years of the 17th century, Middleton wrote topical pamphlets. One – Penniless Parliament of Threadbare Poets was reprinted several times and the subject of a parliamentary inquiry.

These early years writing plays continued to attract controversy. His writing partnership with Thomas Dekker brought him into conflict with Ben Jonson and George Chapman in the so-called War of the Theatres.

His finest work with Dekker was undoubtedly The Roaring Girl, a biography of the notorious Mary Frith.

In the 1610s, Middleton began another playwriting partnership, this time with the actor William Rowley, producing another slew of plays including Wit at Several Weapons and A Fair Quarrel.

The ever adaptable Middleton seemed at ease working with others or by himself. His solo writing credits include the comic masterpiece, A Chaste Maid in Cheapside, in 1613.

In 1620 he was officially appointed as chronologer of the City of London, a post he held until his death.

The 1620s saw the production of his and Rowley's tragedy, and continual favourite, The Changeling, and of several other tragicomedies.

However in 1624, he reached a peak of notoriety when his dramatic allegory A Game at Chess was staged by the King's Men. Though Middleton's approach was strongly patriotic, the Privy Council silenced the play after only nine performances at the Globe theatre, having received a complaint from the Spanish ambassador.

What happened next is a mystery. It is the last play recorded as having being written by Middleton.

Thomas Middleton died at his home at Newington Butts in Southwark in the summer of 1627, and was buried on July 4th, in St Mary's churchyard which today survives as a public park in Elephant and Castle.

John Fletcher was born in December, 1579 in Rye, Sussex. He was baptised on December 20th.

As can be imagined details of much of his life and career have not survived and, accordingly, only a very brief indication of his life and works can be given.

Young Fletcher appears at the very young age of eleven to have entered Corpus Christi College at Cambridge University in 1591. There are no records that he ever took a degree but there is some small evidence that he was being prepared for a career in the church.

However what is clear is that this was soon abandoned as he joined the stream of people who would leave University and decamp to the more bohemian life of commercial theatre in London.

The upbringing of the now teenage Fletcher and his seven siblings now passed to his paternal uncle, the poet and minor official Giles Fletcher. Giles, who had the patronage of the Earl of Essex may have been a liability rather than an advantage to the young Fletcher. With Essex involved in the failed rebellion against Elizabeth Giles was also tainted.

By 1606 John Fletcher appears to have equipped himself with the talents to become a playwright. Initially this appears to have been for the Children of the Queen's Revels, then performing at the Blackfriars Theatre.

Fletcher's early career was marked by one significant failure; The Faithful Shepherdess, his adaptation of Giovanni Battista Guarini's Il Pastor Fido, which was performed by the Blackfriars Children in 1608.

By 1609, however, he had found his stride. With his collaborator John Beaumont, he wrote Philaster, which became a hit for the King's Men and began a profitable association between Fletcher and that company. Philaster appears also to have begun a trend for tragicomedy.

By the middle of the 1610s, Fletcher's plays had achieved a popularity that rivalled Shakespeare's and cemented the pre-eminence of the King's Men in Jacobean London. After his frequent early collaborator John Beaumont's early death in 1616, Fletcher continued working, both singly and in collaboration, until his own death in 1625. By that time, he had produced, or had been credited with, close to fifty plays.

Index of Contents

DRAMATIS PERSONAE
SCENE: Genova
THE NICE VALOUR, or, The Passionate Madman
The **PROLOGUE** at the reviving of this Play
ACTUS PRIMUS
SCÆNA PRIMA
ACTUS SECUNDUS
SCÆNA PRIMA
ACTUS TERTIUS
SCÆNA PRIMA
ACTUS QUARTUS
SCÆNA PRIMA

ACTUS QUINTUS
SCÆNA PRIMA
SCÆNA SECUNDA
SCÆNA TERTIA
EPILOGUE

Duke of Genova.
Shamont his Favourite, a superstitious lover of reputation.
A passionate Lord, the Duke's distracted kinsman.
A Soldier, brother to Shamont.
Lapet, the cowardly Monsieur of Nice Valour.
A Gallant of the same Temper.
Pultrot, } Two Mushroom
Mombazon, } Courtiers.
Two Brothers to the Lady, affecting the passionate Lord.
Four Courtiers.
Jester.
A Priest } In a Masque.
Six Women
Galoshio, a Clown, such another try'd piece of Man's flesh.
WOMEN
Lady, Sister to the Duke, Shamont's beloved.
Lapet's Wife.
A Lady, personating Cupid, Mistriss to the mad Lord.

SCENE: Genova

THE NICE VALOUR, or, The Passionate Madman

The PROLOGUE at the reviving of this Play

It's grown in fashion of late in these days,
To come and beg a sufferance to our Plays
'Faith Gentlemen, our Poet ever writ
Language so good, mixt with such sprightly wit,
He made the Theatre so Sovereign
With his rare Scænes, he scorn'd this crouching vein:
We stabb'd him with keen daggers when we pray'd
Him write a Preface to a Play well made.
He could not write these toyes, 'twas easier far,

To bring a Felon to appear at th' Barr
So much he hated baseness; which this day,
His Scænes will best convince you of in's Play.

[Enter **DUKE, SHAMOUNT, AND FOUR GENTLEMEN**

DUKE
Shamount, welcome; we have mist thee long,
Though absent but two days: I hope your sports
Answer your time and wishes.

SHAMOUNT
Very nobly Sir;
We found game, worthy your delight my Lord,
It was so royal.

DUKE
I've enough to hear on't.
Prethee bestow't upon me in discourse.

FIRST GENTLEMEN
What is this Gentleman, Coz? you are a Courtier,
Therefore know all their insides.

SECOND GENTLEMEN
No farther than the Taffaty goes, good Coz.
For the most part, which is indeed the best part
Of the most general inside; marry thus far
I can with boldness speak this one mans character,
And upon honor, pass it for a true one;
He has that strength of manly merit in him,
That it exceeds his Sovereigns power of gracing;
He's faithfully true to valour, that he hates
The man from Cæsar's time, or farther off,
That ever took disgrace unreveng'd:
And if he chance to read his abject story,
He tears his memory out; and holds it virtuous,
Not to let shame have so much life amongst us;
There is not such a curious piece of courage
Amongst mans fellowship, or one so jealous
Of honors loss, or reputations glory:
There's so much perfect of his growing story.

FIRST GENTLEMEN

'Twould make one dote on virtue as you tell it.

SECOND GENTLEMEN

I have told it to much loss, believe it Coz.

THIRD GENTLEMEN

How the Duke graces him! what is he brother?

FOURTH GENTLEMEN

Do you not yet know him? a vain-glorious coxcomb,
As proud as he that fell for't:
Set but aside his valour, no virtue,
Which is indeed, not fit for any Courtier;
And we his fellows are as good as he,
Perhaps as capable of favour too,
For one thing or another, if 'twere look'd into:
Give me a man, were I a Sovereign now
Has a good stroke at Tennis, and a stiff one,
Can play at Æquinoctium with the Line,
As even, as the thirteenth of September,
When day and night lie in a scale together:
Or may I thrive, as I deserve at Billiards;
No otherwise at Chesse, or at Primero:
These are the parts requir'd, why not advanc'd?

DUKE

Trust me, it was no less than excellent pleasure,
And I'm right glad 'twas thine. How fares our kinsman?
Who can resolve us best?

FIRST GENTLEMEN

I can my Lord.

DUKE

There, if I had a pity without bounds,
It might be all bestowed—A man so lost
In the wild ways of passion, that he's sensible
Of nought, but what torments him?

FIRST GENTLEMEN

True my Lord,
He runs through all the Passions of mankind,
And shifts 'em strangely too: one while in love,
And that so violent, that for want of business,
He'll court the very Prentice of a Laundress,
Though she have kib'd heels: and in's melancholly agen,

He will not brook an Empress though thrice fairer
Than ever Maud was; or higher spirited
Than Cleopatra, or your English Countess:
Then on a suddain he's so merry again,
Out-laughs a Waiting-woman before her first Child:
And turning of a hand, so angry—
Has almost beat the Northern fellow blind;
That is for that use only; if that mood hold my Lord,
Had need of a fresh man; I'll undertake,
He shall bruise three a month.

DUKE
I pity him dearly:
And let it be your charge, with his kind brother
To see his moods observ'd; let every passion
Be fed ev'n to a surfet, which in time
May breed a loathing: let him have enough
Of every object, that his sence is wrapt with;
And being once glutted, then the taste of folly
Will come into his relish.

[Exit.

FIRST GENTLEMEN
I shall see
Your charge my Lord, most faithfully effected:
And how does noble Shamount?

SHAMOUNT
Never ill man
Until I hear of baseness, then I sicken:
I am the healthfull'st man i'th' kingdom else.

[Enter **LAPET.**

FIRST GENTLEMEN
Be armed then for a fit,
Here comes a fellow
Will make you sick at heart, if baseness do't.

SHAMOUNT
Let me be gone: what is he?

FIRST GENTLEMEN
Let me tell you first,
It can be but a qualm: pray stay it out Sir,
Come, y'ave born more than this.

SHAMOUNT
Born? never any thing
That was injurious.

SECOND GENTLEMEN
Ha, I am far from that.

SHAMOUNT
He looks as like a man as I have seen one:
What would you speak of him? speak well I prethee,
Even for humanities cause.

FIRST GENTLEMEN
You'd have it truth though?

SHAMOUNT
What else Sir? I have no reason to wrong heav'n
To favour nature; let her bear her own shame
If she be faulty.

FIRST GENTLEMEN
Monstrous faulty there Sir.

SHAMOUNT
I'm ill at ease already.

FIRST GENTLEMEN
Pray bear up Sir.

SHAMOUNT
I prethee let me take him down with speed then;
Like a wild object that I would not look upon.

FIRST GENTLEMEN
Then thus: he's one that will endure as much
As can be laid upon him.

SHAMOUNT
That may be noble:
I'm kept too long from his acquaintance.

FIRST GENTLEMEN
Oh Sir,
Take heed of rash repentance, y'are too forward
To find out virtue where it never setl'd:
Take the particulars first, of what he endures;
Videlicet, Bastinadoes by the great.

SHAMOUNT
How!

FIRST GENTLEMEN
Thumps by the dozen, and your kicks by wholesale.

SHAMOUNT
No more of him.

FIRST GENTLEMEN
The twinges by the nostril he snuffs up,
And holds it the best remedy for sneezing.

SHAMOUNT
Away.

FIRST GENTLEMEN
H'as been thrice switch'd from 7 a clock till 9.
Yet with a Cart-Horse stomach, fell to breakfast;
Forgetful of his smart.

SHAMOUNT
Nay, the disgrace on't;
There's no smart but that: base things are felt
More by their shames than hurts, Sir. I know you not.
But that you live an injury to nature:
I'm heartily angry with you.

LAPET
Pray give your blow or kick, and begone then:
For I ne'er saw you before; and indeed,
Have nothing to say to you, for I know you not.

SHAMOUNT
Why wouldst thou take a blow?

LAPET
I would not Sir,
Unless 'twere offer'd me; and if from an enemy—
I'd be loth to deny it from a stranger.

SHAMOUNT
What, a blow?
Endure a blow? and shall he live that gives it?

LAPET
Many a fair year—why not Sir?

SHAMOUNT

Let me wonder!
As full a man to see to, and as perfect—
I prethee live not long—

LAPET

How?

SHAMOUNT

Let me intreat it:
Thou dost not know what wrong thou dost mankind,
To walk so long here; not to dye betimes.
Let me advise thee, while thou hast to live here,
Ev'n for man's honour sake, take not a blow more.

LAPET

You should advise them not to strike me then Sir,
For I'll take none I assure you, 'less they are given.

SHAMOUNT

How fain would I preserve mans form from shame
And cannot get it done! however Sir,
I charge thee live not long.

LAPET

This is worse than beating.

SHAMOUNT

Of what profession art thou, tell me Sir,
Besides a Tailor? for I'll know the truth.

LAPET

A Tailor? I'm as good a Gentleman—
Can shew my Arms and all.

SHAMOUNT

How black and blew they are!
Is that your manifestation? upon pain
Of pounding thee to dust, assume not wrongfully
The name of Gentleman, because I'm one,
That must not let thee live.

LAPET

I have done, I have done Sir.
If there be any harm, beshrew the Herald,
I'm sure I ha' not been so long a Gentleman,
To make this anger: I have nothing no where,
But what I dearly pay for.

[Exit.

SHAMOUNT
Groom begone;
I never was so heart-sick yet of man.

[Enter **LADY, THE DUKE'S SISTER, LAPET'S WIFE.**

FIRST GENTLEMEN
Here comes a cordial, Sir, from th'other sex,
Able to make a dying face look chearful.

SHAMOUNT
The blessedness of Ladies—

LADY
Y'are well met Sir.

SHAMOUNT
The sight of you has put an evil from me,
Whose breath was able to make virtue sicken.

LADY
I'm glad I came so fortunately. What was't Sir?

SHAMOUNT
A thing that takes a blow, lives, and eats after it,
In very good health; you ha' not seen the like, Madam,
A Monster worth your sixpence, lovely worth.

FIRST GENTLEMEN
Speak low Sir; by all likely-hoods 'tis her Husband, Lady,
That now bestow'd a visitation on me. Farewel Sir.

[Exit.

SHAMOUNT
Husband? is't possible that he has a wife?
Would any creature have him? 'tis some forc'd match,
If he were not kick'd to th' Church o' th' wedding day,
I'll never come at Court. Can be no otherwise:
Perhaps he was rich, speak mistriss Lapet, was't not so?

WIFE
Nay, that's without all question.

SHAMOUNT

O ho, he would not want kickers enow then;
If you are wise, I much suspect your honesty;
For wisdom never fastens constantly,
But upon merit: if you incline to fool,
You are alike unfit for his society;
Nay, if it were not boldness in the man
That honors you, to advise you, troth his company
Should not be frequent with you.

WIFE
'Tis good counsel Sir.

SHAMOUNT
Oh, I am so careful where I reverence,
So just to goodness, and her precious purity,
I'm as equally jealous, and as fearful,
That any undeserved stain might fall
Upon her sanctified whiteness, as of the sin
That comes by wilfulness.

WIFE
Sir, I love your thoughts,
And honor you for your counsel and your care.

SHAMOUNT
We are your servants.

WIFE
He's but a Gentleman o'th' chamber; he might have kist me:
Faith, where shall one find less courtesie, than at Court?
Say I have an undeserver to my Husband:
That's ne'er the worse for him: well strange lip'd men,
'Tis but a kiss lost, there'll more come agen.

[Exit.

[Enter **THE PASSIONATE LORD, THE DUKESKINSMAN,**

Look, who comes here Sir, his love-fit's upon him:
I know it, by that sett smile, and those congies.
How courteous he's to nothing! which indeed,
Is the next kin to woman; only shadow
The elder Sister of the twain, because 'tis seen too.
See how it kisses the fore-finger still;
Which is the last edition, and being come
So near the thumb, every Cobler has got it.

SHAMOUNT

What a ridiculous piece, humanity
Here makes it self!

FIRST GENTLEMEN
Nay good give leave a little, Sir,
Y'are so precise a manhood—

SHAMOUNT
It afflicts me
When I behold unseemliness in an Image
So near the Godhead, 'tis an injury
To glorious Eternity.

FIRST GENTLEMEN
Pray use patience, Sir.

PASSIONATE LORD
I do confess it freely, precious Lady,
And loves suit is so, the longer it hangs
The worse it is; better cut off, sweet Madam;
Oh, that same drawing in your neather Lip there,
Fore-shews no goodness, Lady; make you question on't?
Shame on me, but I love you.

FIRST GENTLEMEN
Who is't Sir,
You are at all this pains for? may I know her?

PASSIONATE LORD
For thee thou fairest, yet the falsest woman,
That ever broke man's heart-strings.

FIRST GENTLEMEN
How? how's this Sir?

PASSIONATE LORD
What the old trick of Ladies? man's apparel,
Will't ne'er be left amongst you? steal from Court in't?

FIRST GENTLEMEN
I see the Fit grows stronger.

PASSIONATE LORD
Pray let's talk a little.

SHAMOUNT
I can endure no more.

FIRST GENTLEMEN
Good, let's alone a little:
You are so exact a work: love light things somewhat, Sir.

SHAMOUNT
Th'are all but shames.

FIRST GENTLEMEN
What is't you'd say to me, Sir?

PASSIONATE LORD
Can you be so forgetful to enquire it Lady?

FIRST GENTLEMEN
Yes truely, Sir.

PASSIONATE LORD
The more I admire your flintiness:
What cause have I given you, illustrious Madam,
To play this strange part with me?

FIRST GENTLEMEN
Cause enough,
Do but look back Sir, into your memory,
Your love to other women, oh lewd man:
'Tas almost kill'd my heart, you see I'm chang'd with it,
I ha' lost the fashion of my Sex with grief on't,
When I have seen you courting of a Dowdie;
Compar'd with me, and kissing your fore-finger
To one o'th' Black-Guards Mistresses: would not this
Crack a poor Ladies heart, that believ'd love,
And waited for the comfort? but 'twas said, Sir,
A Lady of my hair cannot want pittying:
The Countrey's coming up, farewel to you Sir.

PASSIONATE LORD
Whither intend you, Sir?

FIRST GENTLEMEN
A long journey, Sir:
The truth is, I'm with child, and goe to travel.

PASSIONATE LORD
With child? I never got it.

FIRST GENTLEMEN
I heard you were busie
At the same time, Sir, and was loth to trouble you.

PASSIONATE LORD
Why, are not you a whore then, excellent Madam?

FIRST GENTLEMEN
Oh by no means, 'twas done Sir in the state
Of my belief in you, and that quits me;
It lies upon your falshood.

PASSIONATE LORD
Does it so?
You shall not carry her though Sir, she's my contract.

SHAMOUNT
I prethee, thou four Elements ill brued,
Torment none but thy self; away I say
Thou beast of passion, as the drunkard is
The beast of Wine; dishonor to thy making,
Thou man in fragments.

PASSIONATE LORD
Hear me, precious Madam.

SHAMOUNT
Kneel for thy wits to Heaven.

PASSIONATE LORD
Lady, I'll father it,
Who e'er begot it: 'tis the course of greatness.

SHAMOUNT
How virtue groans at this!

PASSIONATE LORD
I'll raise the Court, but I'll stay your flight.

SHAMOUNT
How wretched is that piece!

[Exit **PASSIONATE LORD.**

FIRST GENTLEMEN
He's the Dukes kinsman, Sir.

SHAMOUNT
That cannot take a passion away, Sir,
Nor cut a Fit, but one poor hour shorter,
He must endure as much as the poorest begger,

That cannot change his money; there's th' equality
In our impartial Essence:
What's the news now?

[Enter a **SERVANT**

SERVANT
Your worthy brother, Sir, 'has left his charge,
And come to see you.

[Enter **SHAMOUNT'S BROTHER, A SOLDIER.**

SHAMOUNT
Oh the noblest welcome
That ever came from man, meet thy deservings:
Methinks I've all joyes treasure in mine arms now.

SOLDIER
You are so fortunate in prevention, brother,
You always leave the answerer barren, Sir,
You comprehend in few words so much worth—

SHAMOUNT
'Tis all too little for thee: come th'art welcome,
So I include all: take especial knowledge pray,
Of this dear Gentleman, my absolute friend,
That loves a Soldier far above a Mistriss,
Thou excellently faithful to 'em both.
But love to manhood, owns the purer troth.

[Exeunt.

ACTUS SECUNDUS

SCÆNA PRIMA

Enter Shamont's brother, a **SOLDIER** and a **LADY**, the Dukes Sister.

LADY
There should be in this Gallery—oh th'are here,
Pray sit down, believe me Sir, I'm weary.

SOLDIER
It well becomes a Lady to complain a little
Of what she never feels: your walk was short, Madam,
You can be but afraid of weariness;

Which well employs the softness of your Sex,
As for the thing it self, you never came to't.

LADY
You're wond'rously well read in Ladies, Sir.

SOLDIER
Shall I think such a creature as you Madam,
Was ever born to feel pain, but in Travel?
There's your full portion,
Besides a little tooth-ach in the breeding,
Which a kind Husband too, takes from you, Madam.

LADY
But where do Ladies, Sir, find such kind Husbands?
Perhaps you have heard
The Rheumatick story of some loving Chandler now,
Or some such melting fellow that you talk
So prodigal of mens kindness: I confess Sir,
Many of those wives are happy, their ambition
Does reach no higher, than to Love and Ignorance,
Which makes an excellent Husband, and a fond one:
Now Sir, your great ones aim at height, and cunning,
And so are oft deceiv'd, yet they must venture it;
For 'tis a Ladies contumely, Sir,
To have a Lord an Ignorant; then the worlds voice
Will deem her for a wanton, e'r she taste on't:
But to deceive a wise man, to whose circumspection,
The world resigns it self, with all his envy;
'Tis less dishonor to us then to fall,
Because his believ'd wisdom keeps out all.

SOLDIER
Would I were the man, Lady, that should venture
His wisdom to your goodness.

LADY
You might fail
In the return, as many men have done, Sir:
I dare not justifie what is to come of me,
Because I know it not, though I hope virtuously;
Marry what's past, or present, I durst put
Into a good mans hand, which if he take
Upon my word for good, it shall not cozen him.

SOLDIER
No, nor hereafter?

LADY

It may hap so too, Sir:
A womans goodness, when she is a wife,
Lies much upon a mans desert, believe it Sir,
If there be fault in her, I'll pawn my life on't,
'Tis first in him, if she were ever good,
That makes one; knowing not a Husband yet,
Or what he may be: I promise no more virtues,
Than I may well perform, for that were cozenage.

SOLDIER

Happy were he that had you with all fears,
That's my opinion, Lady.

[Enter **SHAMOUNT AND A SERVANT** list'ning.

SERVANT

What say you now, Sir?
Dare you give confidence to your own eyes?

SHAMOUNT

Not yet I dare not.

SERVANT

No?

SHAMOUNT

Scarce yet, or yet:
Although I see 'tis he. Why can a thing,
That's but my self divided, be so false?

SERVANT

Nay, do but mark how the chair plays his part too:
How amorously 'tis bent.

SHAMOUNT

Hell take thy bad thoughts,
For they are strange ones. Never take delight
To make a torment worse. Look on 'em heaven,
For that's a brother: send me a fair enemy,
And take him; for a fouler Fiend there breathes not:
I will not sin to think there's ill in her,
But what's of his producing.
Yet goodness, whose inclosure is but flesh,
Holds out oft times but sorrily. But as black Sir,
As ever kindred was: I hate mine own bloud,
Because it is so near thine. Live without honesty,
And mayst thou dye with an unmoist'ned eye,

And no tear follow thee.

[Exit **SHAMONT, SERVANT.**

LADY
Y'are wond'rous merry Sir; I would your Brother heard you.

SOLDIER
Oh my Sister,
I would not out o'th' way, let fall my words Lady,
For the precisest humor.

[Enter **PASSIONATE LORD.**

PASSIONATE LORD
Yea, so close.

SOLDIER
Th'are merry, that's the worst you can report on 'em:
Th'are neither dangerous, nor immodest.

PASSIONATE LORD
So Sir,
Shall I believe you, think you?

SOLDIER
Who's this Lady?

LADY
Oh the Dukes Cosin, he came late from travel, Sir.

SOLDIER
Respect belongs to him.

PASSIONATE LORD
For as I said, Lady,
Th'are merry, that's the worst you can report of 'em:
Th'are neither dangerous, nor immodest.

SOLDIER
How's this?

PASSIONATE LORD
And there I think I left.

SOLDIER
Abuses me.

PASSIONATE LORD
Now to proceed, Lady; perhaps I swore I lov'd you,
If you believe me not, y'are much the wiser.

SOLDIER
He speaks still in my person, and derides me.

PASSIONATE LORD
For I can cog with you.

LADY
You can all do so:
We make no question of mens promptness that way.

PASSIONATE LORD
And smile, and wave a chair with comely grace too,
Play with our Tastle gently, and do fine things,
That catch a Lady sooner than a virtue.

SOLDIER
I never us'd to let man live so long
That wrong'd me.

PASSIONATE LORD
Talk of Battalions, wooe you in a skirmish;
Divine my mind to you Lady; and being sharp set,
Can court you at Half pike: or name your weapon,
We cannot fail you Lady.

[Enter **FIRST GENTLEMAN**

SOLDIER
Now he dies:
Were all succeeding hopes stor'd up within him.

FIRST GENTLEMEN
Oh fie, i'th' Court, Sir?

SOLDIER
I most dearly thank you; Sir.

FIRST GENTLEMEN
'Tis rage ill spent upon a passionate mad man.

SOLDIER
That shall not priviledge him for ever, Sir:
A mad man call you him? I have found too much reason
Sound in his injury to me, to believe him so.

FIRST GENTLEMEN
If ever truth from mans lips may be held
In reputation with you, give this confidence;
And this his Love-fit, which we observe still,
By's flattering and his fineness: at some other time,
He'll go as slovenly as heart can wish.
The love and pity that his Highness shews to him,
Makes every man the more respectful of him:
Has never a passion, but is well provided for,
As this of Love, he is full fed in all
His swinge, as I may tearm it: have but patience,
And ye shall witness somewhat.

SOLDIER
Still he mocks me:
Look you, in action, in behaviour, Sir;
Hold still the chair, with a grand mischief to you,
Or I'll let so much strength upon your heart, Sir—

PASSIONATE LORD
I feel some power has restrain'd me Lady:
If it be sent from Love, say, I obey it,
And ever keep a voice to welcome it.

SONG.
Thou Deity, swift winged Love,
Sometimes below, sometimes above,
Little in shape, but great in power,
Thou that mak'st a heart thy Tower,
And thy loop-holes Ladies eyes,
From whence thou strik'st the fond and wise.
Did all the Shafts in thy fair Quiver
Stick fast in my ambitious Liver;
Yet thy power would I adore.
And call upon thee to shoot more,
Shoot more, shoot more.

[Enter one like a **CUPID**, offering to shoot at him.

PASSIONATE LORD
I prethee hold though, sweet Celestial boy;
I'm not requited yet with love enough,
For the first Arrow that I have within me;
And if thou be an equal Archer Cupid,
Shoot this Lady, and twenty more for me.

LADY

Me Sir?

FIRST GENTLEMEN
'Tis nothing but device, fear it not Lady;
You may be as good a Maid after that shaft, Madam,
As e'er your mother was at twelve and a half:
'Tis like the boy that draws it, 'tas no sting yet.

CUPID
'Tis like the miserable Maid that draws it—Aside.
That sees no comfort yet, seeing him so passionate.

PASSIONATE LORD
Strike me the Duchess of Valois in love with me,
With all the speed thou canst, and two of her Women.

CUPID
You shall have more.

[Exit.

PASSIONATE LORD
Tell 'em I tarry for 'em.

FIRST GENTLEMEN
Who would be angry with that walking trouble now?
That hurts none but it self?

SOLDIER
I am better quieted.

PASSIONATE LORD
I'll have all women-kind struck in time for me
After thirteen once:
I see this Cupid will not let me want,
And let him spend his forty shafts an hour,
They shall be all found from the Dukes Exchequer;
He's come already.

SONG
Oh turn thy bow,
Thy power we feel and know,
Fair Cupid turn away thy Bow:
They be those golden Arrows,
Bring Ladies all their sorrows,
And till there be more truth in men,
Never shoot at Maid agen.

PASSIONATE LORD
What a felicity of whores are here!
And all my Concubines struck bleeding new:
A man can in his life time make but one woman,
But he may make his fifty Queans a month.

CUPID
Have you remembred a Priest, honest brothers?

FIRST BROTHER
Yes Sister, and this is the young Gentleman,
Make you no question of our faithfulness.

SECOND BROTHER
His growing shame, Sister, provokes our care:

PRIEST
He must be taken in this fit of Love, Gentlemen.

FIRST BROTHER
What else Sir, he shall do't.

SECOND BROTHER
Enough.

FIRST BROTHER
Be chearful wench.

[A dance. **CUPID** leading.

PASSIONATE LORD
Now by the stroke of pleasure, a deep oath,
Nimbly hopt Ladies all; what height they bear too!
A story higher than your common statures;
A little man must go up stairs to kiss 'em:
What a great space there is
Betwixt Loves Dining Chamber, and his Garret!
I'll try the utmost height—the Garret stoops methinks;
The rooms are made all bending, I see that,
And not so high as a man takes 'em for.

CUPID
Now if you'll follow me Sir, I've that power,
To make them follow you.

PASSIONATE LORD
Are they all shot?

CUPID
All, all Sir, every mothers daughter of 'em.

PASSIONATE LORD
Then there's no fear of following; if they be once shot
They'll follow a man to th' devil—As for you, Sir—

[Exit with the **LADY** and the **MASQUERS**.

SOLDIER
Me Sir?

FIRST GENTLEMEN
Nay sweet Sir.

SOLDIER
A noise, a threatening, did you not hear it Sir?

FIRST GENTLEMEN
Without regard, Sir, so would I hear you.

SOLDIER
This must come to something, never talk of that Sir.
You never saw it otherwise.

FIRST GENTLEMEN
Nay dear merit—

SOLDIER
Me above all men?

FIRST GENTLEMEN
Troth you wrong your anger.

SOLDIER
I will be arm'd, my honourable Letcher.

FIRST GENTLEMEN
Oh fie sweet Sir.

SOLDIER
That devours womens honesties by lumps,
And never chaw'st thy pleasure:

SECOND GENTLEMEN
What do you mean, Sir?

SOLDIER

What does he mean t'ingross all to himself?
There's others love a whore as well as he Sir.

FIRST GENTLEMEN
Oh, if that be part o' th' fury, we have a City
Is very well provided for that case;
Let him alone with her, Sir, we have Women
Are very charitable to proper men,
And to a Soldier that has all his limbs;
Marry the sick and lame gets not a penny:
Right womens charity, and the Husbands follow't too:
Here comes his Highness Sir.

[Enter **DUKE AND LORDS**

SOLDIER
I'll walk to cool my self.

[Exit.

DUKE
Who's that?

FIRST GENTLEMEN
The brother of Shamont.

DUKE
He's Brother then
To all the Courts love, they that love discreetly,
And place their friendliness upon desert:
As for the rest, that with a double face
Look upon merit much like fortunes visage,
That looks two ways, both to life's calms and storms,
I'll so provide for him, chiefly for him,
He shall not wish their loves, nor dread their envies.
And here comes my Shamont.

[Enter **SHAMOUNT**

SHAMOUNT
That Ladies virtues are my only joyes,
And he to offer to lay siege to them?

DUKE
Shamont.

SHAMOUNT
Her goodness is my pride: in all discourses,

As often as I hear rash tongu'd gallants,
Speak rudely of a woman, presently
I give in but her name, and th'are all silent:
Oh who would loose this benefit?

DUKE
Come hither Sir.

SHAMOUNT
'Tis like the Gift of Healing, but Diviner;
For that but cures diseases in the body,
This works a cure on Fame, on Reputation:
The noblest piece of Surgery upon earth.

DUKE
Shamont; he minds me not.

SHAMOUNT
A Brother do't?

DUKE
Shamont I say.

[Gives him a touch with his switch.

SHAMOUNT
Ha?
If he be mortal, by this hand he perishes;

[Draws.

Unless it be a stroke from heaven, he dies for't.

DUKE
Why, how now Sir? 'twas I.

SHAMOUNT
The more's my misery.

DUKE
Why, what's the matter prethee?

SHAMOUNT
Can you ask it, Sir?
No man else should; stood forty lives before him,
By this I would have op'd my way to him;
It could not be you Sir, excuse him not,
What e'er he be, as y'are dear to honor,

That I may find my peace agen.

DUKE
Forbear I say,
Upon my love to truth, 'twas none but I.

SHAMOUNT
Still miserable?

DUKE
Come, come, what ails you Sir?

SHAMOUNT
Never sate shame cooling so long upon me,
Without a satisfaction in revenge,
And heaven has made it here a sin to wish it.

DUKE
Hark you Sir!

SHAMOUNT
Oh y'ave undone me.

DUKE
How?

SHAMOUNT
Cruelly undone me;
I have lost my peace and reputation by you:
Sir, pardon me, I can never love you more.

[Exit.

DUKE
What language call you this Sirs?

FIRST GENTLEMEN
Truth my Lord, I've seldom heard a stranger—

SECOND GENTLEMEN
He is a man of a most curious valour,
Wondrous precise, and punctual in that virtue.

DUKE
But why to me so punctual? my last thought
Was most intirely fixt on his advancement
Why, I came now to put him in possession
Of his fair fortunes: what a mis-conceiver 'tis!

And from a Gentleman of our Chamber meerly,
Made him Vice-Admiral: I was setled in't.
I love him next to health: call him Gentlemen;
Why would not you, or you, ha' taken as much,
And never murmur'd?

[Exit **FIRST GENTLEMEN**

SECOND GENTLEMEN
Troth, I think we should, my Lord,
And there's a fellow walks about the Court,
Would take a hundred of 'em.

DUKE
I hate you all for't,
And rather praise his high pitch'd fortitude,
Though in extreams for niceness: now I think on't,
I would I had never done't—Now Sir, where is he?

[Enter **FIRST GENTLEMEN.**

FIRST GENTLEMEN
His sute is only Sir, to be excus'd.

DUKE
He shall not be excus'd, I love him dearlier:
Say we intreat him; goe, he must not leave us

[Exit **TWO GENTLEMEN.**

So virtue bless me, I ne'er knew him paralell'd;
Why, he's more precious to me now, than ever.

[Enter **GENTLEMEN, AND SHAMONT.**

SECOND GENTLEMEN
With much fair language w'ave brought him.

DUKE
Thanks—Where is he?

SECOND GENTLEMEN
Yonder Sir.

DUKE
Come forward man.

SHAMOUNT

Pray pardon me, I'm asham'd to be seen Sir.

DUKE
Was ever such a touchie man heard of?
Prethee come nearer.

SHAMOUNT
More into the light?
Put not such cruelty into your requests my Lord,
First to disgrace me publickly, and then draw me
Into mens eye-sight, with the shame yet hot
Upon my reputation.

DUKE
What disgrace, Sir?

SHAMOUNT
What?
Such as there can be no forgiveness for,
That I can find in honour.

DUKE
That's most strange, Sir.

SHAMOUNT
Yet I have search'd my bosom to find one,
And wrestled with my inclination,
But 'twill not be: would you had kill'd me Sir.
With what an ease had I forgiven you then!
But to endure a stroke from any hand
Under a punishing Angel, which is justice,
Honor disclaim that man, for my part chiefly:
Had it been yet the malice of your sword,
Though it had cleft me, 't had been noble to me;
You should have found my thanks paid in a smile
If I had fell unworded; but to shame me,
With the correction that your horse should have,
Were you ten thousand times my royal Lord,
I cannot love you never, nor desire to serve you more.
If your drum call me, I am vowed to valour,
But peace shall never know me yours agen,
Because I've lost mine own, I speak to dye Sir;
Would you were gracious that way to take off shame,
With the same swiftness as you pour it on:
And since it is not in the power of Monarchs
To make a Gentleman, which is a substance
Only begot of merit, they should be careful
Not to destroy the worth of one so rare,

Which neither they can make; nor lost, repair.

[Exit.

DUKE
Y'ave set a fair light Sir before my judgement,
Which burns with wondrous clearness; I acknowledge it,
And your worth with it: but then Sir, my love,
My love—what gone agen?

FIRST GENTLEMEN
And full of scorn, my Lord.

DUKE
That language will undoe the man that keeps it.
Who knows no diff'rence 'twixt contempt and manhood.
Upon your love to goodness, Gentlemen,
Let me not lose him long: how now?

[Enter a **HUNTSMAN.**

HUNTSMAN
The game's at height my Lord.

DUKE
Confound both thee and it: hence break it off;
He hates me brings me news of any pleasure:
I felt not such a conflict since I cou'd;
Distinguish betwixt worthiness and bloud.

[Exit

ACTUS TERTIUS

SCÆNA PRIMA

[Enter the **TWO BROTHERS, FIRST GENTLEMAN**

FIRST GENTLEMEN
I heartily commend your project, Gentlemen,
'Twas wise and virtuous.

FIRST BROTHER
'Twas for the safety
Of precious honour Sir, which near bloud binds us to:
He promis'd the poor easie fool there, marriage,

There was a good Maiden-head lost i'th' belief on't,
Beshrew her hasty confidence.

FIRST GENTLEMEN
Oh no more, Sir,
You make her weep agen; alas poor Cupid:
Shall she not shift her self?

FIRST BROTHER
Oh by no means Sir:
We dare not have her seen yet, all the while
She keeps this shape, 'tis but thought device,
And she may follow him so without suspition,
To see if she can draw all his wild passions,
To one point only, and that's love, the main point:
So far his Highness grants, and gave at first,
Large approbation to the quick conceit,
Which then was quick indeed.

FIRST GENTLEMEN
You make her blush insooth.

FIRST BROTHER
I fear 'tis more the flag of shame, than grace Sir.

FIRST GENTLEMEN
They both give but one kind of colour, Sir:
If it be bashfulness in that kind taken,
It is the same with grace; and there she weeps agen.
In truth y'are too hard, much, much too bitter Sir,
Unless you mean to have her weep her eyes out,
To play a Cupid truly.

FIRST BROTHER
Come ha' done then:
We should all fear to sin first; for 'tis certain,
When 'tis once lodg'd, though entertain'd in mirth,
It must be wept out, if it e'er come forth.

FIRST GENTLEMEN
Now 'tis so well, I'll leave you.

FIRST BROTHER
Faithfully welcome, Sir,
Go Cupid to your charge; he's your own now;
If he want love, none will be blam'd but you.

CUPID

The strangest marriage, and unfortunat'st Bride
That ever humane memory contain'd;
I cannot be my self for't.

[Exit.

[Enter the **CLOWN**

CLOWN
Oh Gentlemen?

FIRST BROTHER
How now, Sir, what's the matter?

CLOWN
His melancholly passion is half spent already,
Then comes his angry fit at the very tail on't,
Then comes in my pain, gentlemen; h'as beat me e'en to a
Cullis. I am nothing, right worshipful, but very pap,
And jelly: I have no bones, my body's all one business,
They talk of ribs and chines most freely abroad i'th' world,
Why, I have no such thing; who ever lives to see me dead,
Gentlemen, shall find me all mummie good to fill Gallipots,
And long dildo glasses: I shall not have a bone to throw
At a dog.

OMNES
Alas poor vassal; how he goes!

CLOWN
Oh Gentlemen,
I am unjoynted, do but think o' that:
My breast is beat into my maw, that what I eat,
I am fain to take't in all at mouth with spoons;
A lamentable hearing; and 'tis well known, my belly
Is driven into my back.
I earn'd four Crowns a month most dearly Gentlemen,
And one he must have when the fit's upon him,
The Privy-purse allows it, and 'tis thriftiness,
He would break else some forty pounds in Casements,
And in five hundred years undo the Kingdom:
I have cast it up to a quarrel.

FIRST BROTHER
There's a fellow kickt about Court, I would
He had his place, brother, but for one fit of his indignation.

SECOND BROTHER

And suddainly I have thought upon a means for't.

FIRST BROTHER
I prethee how?

SECOND BROTHER
'Tis but preferring, Brother
This stockfish to his service, with a Letter
Of commendations, the same way he wishes it,
And then you win his heart: for o' my knowledge
He has laid wait this half year for a fellow
That will be beaten, and with a safe conscience
We may commend the carriage of this man in't;
Now servants he has kept, lusty tall feeders,
But they have beat him, and turn'd themselves away:
Now one that would endure, is like to stay,
And get good wages of him; and the service too
Is ten times milder, Brother, I would not wish it else.
I see the fellow has a sore crush'd body,
And the more need he has to be kick'd at ease.

CLOWN
I sweet Gentlemen, a kick of ease, send me to such a Master.

SECOND BROTHER
No more I say, we have one for thee, a soft footed Master,
One that wears wooll in's toes.

CLOWN
Oh Gentlemen, soft garments may you wear,
Soft skins may you wed,
But as plump as pillows, both for white and red.
And now will I reveal a secret to you,
Since you provide for my poor flesh so tenderly,
Has hir'd meer rogues out of his chamber window,
To beat the Soldier, Monsieur Shamont's Brother:

FIRST BROTHER
That nothing concerns us, Sir.

CLOWN
For no cause, Gentlemen,
Unless it be for wearing Shoulder-points,
With longer taggs than his.

SECOND BROTHER
Is not that somewhat?
Birlakin Sir, the difference of long taggs,

Has cost many a man's life, and advanc'd other some,
Come follow me.

CLOWN
See what a gull am I:
Oh every man in his profession;
I know a thump now as judiciously,
As the proudest he that walks, I'll except none;
Come to a tagg, how short I fall! I'm gone

[Exeunt.

[Enter **LAPET.**

LAPET
I have been ruminating with my self,
What honor a man loses by a kick:
Why; what's a kick? the fury of a foot,
Whose indignation commonly is stampt
Upon the hinder quarter of a man:
Which is a place very unfit for honor,
The world will confess so much:
Then what disgrace I pray, does that part surfer
Where honor never comes, I'de fain know that?
This being well forc'd, and urg'd, may have the power
To move most Gallants to take kicks in time,
And spurn out the duelloes out o' th' kingdom,
For they that stand upon their honor most,
When they conceive there is no honor lost,
As by a Table that I have invented
For that purpose alone, shall appear plainly,
Which shews the vanity of all blows at large.
And with what ease they may be took of all sides,
Numbring but twice o'er the Letters patience
From C. P. to E. I doubt not but in small time
To see a dissolution of all bloud-shed,
If the reform'd Kick do but once get up:
For what a lamentable folly 'tis,
If we observe't, for every little justle,
Which is but the ninth part of a sound thump,
In our meek computation, we must fight forsooth, yes,
If I kill, I'm hang'd; if I be kill'd my self,
I dye for't also: is not this trim wisdom?
Now for the Con, a man may be well beaten,
Yet pass away his fourscore years smooth after:
I had a Father did it, and to my power
I will not be behind him.

[Enter **SHAMOUNT**

SHAMOUNT
Oh well met.

LAPET
Now a fine punch or two, I look for't duly.

SHAMOUNT
I've been to seek you.

LAPET
Let me know your Lodging, Sir,
I'll come to you once a day, and use your pleasure, Sir.

SHAMOUNT
I'm made the fittest man for thy society:
I'll live and dye with thee, come shew me a chamber;
There is no house but thine, but only thine,
That's fit to cover me: I've took a blow, sirrah.

LAPET
I would you had indeed: why, you may see, Sir;
You'll all come to't in time, when my Book's out.

SHAMOUNT
Since I did see thee last, I've took a blow.

LAPET
Pha Sir, that's nothing: I ha' took forty since.

SHAMOUNT
What? and I charg'd thee thou shouldst not?

LAPET
I Sir, you might charge your pleasure.
But they would give't me, whether I would or no.

SHAMOUNT
Oh, I walk without my peace, I've no companion now;
Prethee resolve me, for I cannot aske
A man more beaten to experience,
Than thou art in this kind, what manner of blow
Is held the most disgraceful, or distasteful?
For thou dost only censure 'em by the hurt,
Not by the shame they do thee: yet having felt
Abuses of all kinds, thou may'st deliver,
Though't be by chance, the most injurious one.

LAPET
You put me to't, Sir; but to tell you truth,
They're all as one with me, little exception.

SHAMOUNT
That little may do much, let's have it from you.

LAPET
With all the speed I may, first then, and foremost,
I hold so reverently of the Bastinado, Sir,
That if it were the dearest friend i'th' world,
I'de put it into his hand.

SHAMOUNT
Go too, I'll pass that then.

LAPET
Y'are the more happy, Sir,
Would I were past it too:
But being accustom'd to't. It is the better carried.

SHAMOUNT
Will you forward?

LAPET
Then there's your souce, your wherit and your dowst,
Tugs on the hair, your bob o'th' lips, a whelp on't,
I ne'er could find much difference: Now your thump,
A thing deriv'd first from your Hemp-beaters,
Takes a mans wind away, most spitefully:
There's nothing that destroys a Collick like it,
For't leaves no wind i'th' body.

SHAMOUNT
On Sir, on.

LAPET
Pray give me leave, I'm out of breath with thinking on't.

SHAMOUNT
This is far off yet.

LAPET
For the twinge by th' nose,
'Tis certainly unsightly, so my Table says,
But helps against the head-ach, wond'rous strangely.

SHAMOUNT

Is't possible?

LAPET

Oh your crush'd nostrils slakes your opilation,
And makes your pent powers flush to wholsome sneezes.

SHAMOUNT

I never thought there had been half that virtue
In a wrung nose before.

LAPET

Oh plenitude, Sir:
Now come we lower to our modern Kick,
Which has been mightily in use of late,
Since our young men drank Coltsfoot: and I grant you,
'Tis a most scornful wrong, cause the foot plays it;
But mark agen, how we that take't, requite it
With the like scorn, for we receive it backward;
And can there be a worse disgrace retorted?

SHAMOUNT

And is this all?

LAPET

All but a Lug by th' ear,
Or such a trifle.

SHAMOUNT

Happy sufferer,
All this is nothing to the wrong I bear:
I see the worst disgrace, thou never felt'st yet;
It is so far from thee thou canst not think on't;
Nor dare I let thee know, it is so abject.

LAPET

I would you would though, that I might prepare for't
For I shall ha't at one time or another:
If't be a thwack, I make account of that;
There's no new fashion'd swap that e'er came up yet,
But I've the first on 'em, I thank 'em for't.

[Enter **LADY AND SERVANTS.**

LADY

Hast thou enquir'd?

FIRST SERVANT

But can hear nothing, Madam.

SHAMOUNT
If there be but so much substance in thee
To make a shelter for a man disgrac'd,
Hide my departure from that glorious woman
That comes with all perfection about her:
So noble, that I dare not be seen of her,
Since shame took hold of me: upon thy life
No mention of me.

LAPET
I'll cut out my tongue first,
Before I'll loose my life, there's more belongs to't.

LADY
See there's a Gentleman, enquire of him.

SECOND SERVANT
For Monsieur Shamont, Madam?

LADY
For whom else, Sir?

FIRST SERVANT
Why, this fellow dares not see him.

LADY
How?

FIRST SERVANT
Shamont, Madam?
His very name's worse than a Feaver to him,
And when he cries, there's nothing stills him sooner;
Madam, your Page of thirteen is too hard for him,
'Twas try'd i'th' wood-yard.

LADY
Alas poor grieved Merit!
What is become of him? if he once fail,
Virtue shall find small friendship: farewel then
To Ladies worths, for any hope in men,
He lov'd for goodness, not for Wealth, or Lust,
After the world's foul dotage, he ne'er courted
The body, but the beauty of the mind,
A thing which common courtship never thinks on:
All his affections were so sweet and fair,
There is no hope for fame if he despair.

[Exit **LADY**, **SERVANT**.

[Enter the **CLOWN**. He kicks **LAPET**.

LAPET
Good morrow to you agen most heartily, Sir,
Cry you mercy, I heard you not, I was somewhat busie.

CLOWN
He takes it as familiarly, as an Ave,
Or precious salutation: I was sick till I had one,
Because I am so us'd to't.

LAPET
However you deserve, your friends and mine, here
Give you large commendations i'this Letter,
They say you will endure well.

CLOWN
I'de be loath
To prove 'em liers: I've endur'd as much
As mortal pen and ink can set me down for.

LAPET
Say you me so?

CLOWN
I know and feel it so, Sir,
I have it under Black and White already;
I need no Pen to paint me out.

LAPET
He fits me,
And hits my wishes pat, pat: I was ne'er
In possibility to be better mann'd,
For he's half lam'd already, I see't plain,
But take no notice on't, for fear I make
The rascal proud, and dear, to advance his wages;
First, let me grow into particulars with you;
What have you endured of worth? let me hear.

CLOWN
Marry Sir, I'm almost beaten blind.

LAPET
That's pretty well for a beginning,
But many a Mill-horse has endur'd as much.

CLOWN
Shame o'th' Millers heart for his unkindness then.

LAPET
Well Sir, what then?

CLOWN
I've been twice thrown down stairs, just before supper.

LAPET
Puh, so have I, that's nothing.

CLOWN
I but Sir,
Was yours pray before supper?

LAPET
There thou posest me.

CLOWN
I marry, that's it, 't had been less grief to me,
Had I but fill'd my belly, and then tumbled,
But to be flung down fasting, there's the dolour.

LAPET
It would have griev'd me, that indeed: proceed Sir.

CLOWN
I have been pluck'd and tugg'd by th' hair o'th' head
About a Gallery, half an Acre long.

LAPET
Yes, that's a good one, I must needs confess,
A principal good one that, an absolute good one,
I have been trode upon, and spurn'd about,
But never tugg'd by th' hair, I thank my fates.

CLOWN
Oh 'tis a spiteful pain.

LAPET
Peace, never speak on't,
For putting men in mind on't.

CLOWN
To conclude,
I'm bursten Sir: my belly will hold no meat.

LAPET

No? that makes amends for all.

CLOWN

Unless 't be puddings,
Or such fast food, any loose thing beguiles me, I'm ne'er the better
for't.

LAPET

Sheeps-heads will stay with thee?

CLOWN

Yes Sir, or Chaldrons.

LAPET

Very well sir:
Your bursten fellows must take heed of surfets:
Strange things it seems, you have endur'd;

CLOWN

Too true Sir.

LAPET

But now the question is, what you will endure
Hereafter in my service?

CLOWN

Anything
That shall be reason Sir, for I'm but froth;
Much like a thing new calv'd, or come more nearer Sir,
Y'ave seen a cluster of Frog-spawns in April,
E'en such a starch am I, as weak and tender
As a green woman yet.

LAPET

Now I know this,
I will be very gently angry with thee,
And kick thee carefully.

CLOWN

Oh I, sweet Sir.

LAPET

Peace, when thou art offer'd well, lest I begin now.
Your friends and mine have writ here for your truth,
They'll pass their words themselves, and I must meet 'em.

CLOWN
Then have you all:

[Exit.

As for my honesty, there is no fear of that,
For I have ne'er a whole bone about me.

[Exit.

[Enter the passionate **COSIN**, rudely, and carelesly apparrell'd, unbrac'd, and untruss'd. The **CUPID** following.

CUPID
Think upon love, which makes all creatures handsome,
Seemly for eye-sight; goe not so diffusedly,
There are great Ladies purpose Sir to visit you.

PASSIONATE LORD
Grand plagues, shut in my casements, that the breaths
Of their Coach-mares reek not into my nostrils;
Those beasts are but a kind of bawdy fore-runners.

CUPID
It is not well with you,
When you speak ill of fair Ladies.

PASSIONATE LORD
Fair mischiefs, give me a nest of Owls and take 'em;
Happy is he, say I, whose window opens
To a brown Bakers chimney, he shall be sure there
To hear the Bird sometimes after twilight:
What a fine thing 'tis methinks to have our garments
Sit loose upon us thus, thus carelesly,
It is more manly, and more mortifying;
For we're so much the readier for our shrouds:
For how ridiculous wer't, to have death come,
And take a fellow, pinn'd up like a Mistriss!
About his neck a Ruff, like a pinch'd Lanthorn,
Which School-boys make in winter; and his doublet
So close and pent, as if he fear'd one prison
Would not be strong enough, to keep his soul in;
But's Tailor makes another:
And trust me; (for I know't when I lov'd Cupid,)
He does endure much pain, for the poor praise
Of a neat sitting suit.

CUPID

One may be handsome, Sir,
And yet not pain'd, nor proud.

PASSIONATE LORD
There you lie Cupid,
As bad as Mercury: there is no handsomness,
But has a wash of Pride and Luxury,
And you go there too Cupid. Away dissembler,
Thou tak'st the deeds part, which befools us all;
Thy Arrow heads shoot out sinners: hence away,
And after thee I'll send a powerful charm,
Shall banish thee for ever.

CUPID
Never, never,
I am too sure thine own.

[Exit.

PASSIONATE LORD [Sings]
Hence all you vain Delights,
As short as are the nights,
Wherein you spend your folly,
There's nought in this life sweet,
If man were wise to see't,
But only melancholly,
Oh sweetest melancholly.
Welcome folded Arms, and fixed Eyes,
A sigh that piercing mortifies,
A look that's fastened to the ground,
A tongue chain'd up without a sound.

Fountain heads, and pathless Groves,
Places which pale passion loves:
Moon-light walks, when all the Fowls
Are warmly hous'd, save Bats and Owls;
A mid-night Bell, a parting groan,
These are the sounds we feed upon;
Then stretch our bones in a still gloomy valley,
Nothing's so dainty sweet, as lovely melancholly.

[Exit.

[Enter at another door **LAPET**, the **CUPID'S BROTHER'S** watching his coming.

FIRST BROTHER
So, so, the Woodcock's ginn'd;
Keep this door fast brother.

SECOND BROTHER
I'll warrant this.

FIRST BROTHER
I'll goe incense him instantly;
I know the way to't.

SECOND BROTHER
Will't not be too soon think you,
And make two fits break into one?

FIRST BROTHER
Pah, no, no; the tail of his melancholy
Is always the head of his anger, and follows as close,
As the Report follows the powder.

LAPET
This is the appointed place, and the hour struck,
If I can get security for's truth,
I'll never mind his honesty, poor worm,
I durst lay him by my wife, which is a benefit
Which many Masters ha' not: I shall ha' no Maid
Now got with child, but what I get my self,
And that's no small felicity: in most places
Th'are got by th' Men, and put upon the Masters,
Nor shall I be resisted when I strike,
For he can hardly stand; these are great blessings.

PASSIONATE LORD
I want my food, deliver me a Varlet.   Within.

LAPET
How now, from whence comes that?

PASSIONATE LORD
I am allow'd a carkass to insult on;
Where's the villain?

LAPET
He means not me I hope.

PASSIONATE LORD
My maintenance rascals; my bulk, my exhibition.

LAPET
Bless us all,
What names are these? Would I were gone agen.

[The passionate **MAN** enters in fury with a Truncheon.

[He Sings.
A curse upon thee for a slave,
Art thou here, and heardst me rave?
Fly not sparkles from mine eye,
To shew my indignation nigh?
Am I not all foam, and fire,
With voice as hoarse as a Town-crier?
How my back opes and shuts together,
With fury, as old mens with weather!
Could'st thou not hear my teeth gnash hither?

LAPET
No truly, Sir, I thought 't had been a Squirrel,
Shaving a Hazel-nut.

PASSIONATE LORD
Death, Hell, Fiends, and darkness.
I will thrash thy maungy carkass.

LAPET
Oh sweet Sir.

PASSIONATE LORD
There cannot be too many tortures,
Spent upon those louzie Quarters.

LAPET
Hold, oh.
Falls down for dead.

PASSIONATE LORD
Thy bones shall rue, thy bones shall rue.

[Sings again.
Thou nasty, scurvy, mongril Toad,
Mischief on thee;
Light upon thee,
All the plagues
That can confound thee
Or did ever raign abroad:
Better a thousand lives it cost,
Than have brave anger spilt or lost.

[Exit.

LAPET
May I open mine eyes yet, and safely peep:
I'll try a groon first—oh—Nay then he's gone.
There was no other policy but to dy,
He would ha' made me else. Ribs are you sore?
I was ne'er beaten to a tune before.

[Enter the **TWO BROTHERS**

FIRST BROTHER
Lapet.

LAPET
Agen? Falls again.

FIRST BROTHER
Look, look, he's flat agen,
And stretched out like a Coarse, a handful longer
Than he walks, trust me brother. Why Lapet
I hold my life we shall not get him speak now:
Monsieur Lapet; it must be a privy token,
If any thing fetch him, he's so far gone.
We come to pass our words for your mans truth.

LAPET
Oh Gentlemen y'are welcome: I have been thrash'd i' faith.

SECOND BROTHER
How? thrash'd Sir?

LAPET
Never was Shrove-tuesday Bird
So cudgell'd, Gentlemen.

FIRST BROTHER
Pray how? by whom Sir?

LAPET
Nay, that I know not.

FIRST BROTHER
Not who did this wrong?

LAPET
Only a thing came like a Walking Song.

FIRST BROTHER
What beaten with a Song?

LAPET
Never more tightly, Gentlemen:
Such crotchets happen now and then, methinks
He that endures well, of all waters drinks.

[Exeunt.

Enter **SHAMOUNT'S BROTHER, THE SOLDIER, AND FIRST GENTLEMEN**

SOLDIER
Yes, yes, this was a Madman, Sir, with you,
A passionate Mad-man.

FIRST GENTLEMEN
Who would ha' lookt for this, Sir?

SOLDIER
And must be priviledg'd: a pox priviledge him:
I was never so dry beaten since I was born,
And by a litter of rogues, meer rogues, the whole twenty
Had not above nine elbows amongst 'em all too:
And the most part of those left-handed rascals,
The very vomit, Sir, of Hospitals,
Bridewels, and Spittle-houses; such nasty smellers,
That if they'd been unfurnish'd of Club-Truncheons,
They might have cudgell'd me with their very stinks,
It was so strong, and sturdy: and shall this,
This filthy injury, be set off with madness?

FIRST GENTLEMEN
Nay, take your own blouds counsel, Sir, hereafter,
I'll deal no further in't: if you remember,
It was not come to blows, when I advis'd you.

SOLDIER
No, but I ever said, 'twould come to something,
And 'tis upon me, thank him: were he kin
To all the mighty Emperors upon earth,
He has not now in life three hours to reckon;
I watch but a free time.

[Enter **SHAMOUNT**

FIRST GENTLEMEN
Your noble brother, Sir, I'll leave you now.

[Exit

SHAMOUNT
Soldier, I would I could perswade my thoughts
From thinking thee a brother, as I can
My tongue from naming on't: thou hast no friend here,
But fortune and thy own strength, trust to them.

SOLDIER
How? what's the incitement, sir?

SHAMOUNT
Treachery to virtue;
Thy treachery, thy faithless circumvention:
Has Honor so few daughters, never fewer,
And must thou aim thy treachery at the best?
The very front of virtue, that blest Lady? the Dukes Sister?
Created more for admirations cause,
Than for loves ends; whose excellency sparkles
More in Divinity, than mortal beauty;
And as much difference 'twixt her mind and body,
As 'twixt this earths poor centre, and the Sun:
And could'st thou be so injurious to fair goodness,
Once to attempt to court her down to frailty?
Or put her but in mind that there is weakness,
Sin, and desire, which she should never hear of?
Wretch, thou'st committed worse than Sacriledge,
In the attempting on't, and ought'st to dye for't.

SOLDIER
I rather ought to do my best, to live, Sir.
Provoke me not; for I've a wrong sits on me,
That makes me apt for mischief; I shall lose
All respects suddainly of friendship, Brother-hood,
Or any sound that way.

SHAMOUNT
But 'ware me most;
For I come with a two-edg'd injury;
Both my disgrace, and thy apparent falshood,
Which must be dangerous.

SOLDIER

I courted her, Sir;
Love starve me with delays, when I confess it not.

SHAMOUNT
There's nothing then but death
Can be a pennance fit for that confession.

SOLDIER
But far from any vitious taint.

SHAMOUNT
Oh Sir,
Vice is a mighty stranger grown to courtship.

SOLDIER
Nay, then the fury of my wrong light on thee.

[Enter **FIRST GENTLEMEN AND OTHERS**

FIRST GENTLEMEN
Forbear, the Duke's at hand.
Here, hard at hand, upon my reputation.

SOLDIER
I must do something now.

[Exit **SOLDIER**.

SHAMOUNT
I'll follow you close Sir.

FIRST GENTLEMEN
We must intreat you must not; for the Duke
Desires some conference with you.

SHAMOUNT
Let me go,
As y'are Gentlemen.

SECOND GENTLEMEN
Faith we dare not Sir.

SHAMOUNT
Dare ye be false to honor, and yet dare not
Do a man justice? give me leave—

FIRST GENTLEMEN
Good sweet Sir.

H'as sent twice for you.

SHAMOUNT
Is this brave, or manly?

FIRST GENTLEMEN
I prethee be conform'd.

SHAMOUNT
Death—

[Enter **DUKE**.

SECOND GENTLEMEN
Peace, he's come in troth.

SHAMOUNT
Oh have you betraid me to my shame afresh?
How am I bound to loath you!

DUKE
Shamont, welcome,
I sent twice.

SECOND GENTLEMEN
But my Lord, he never heard on't.

SHAMOUNT
Pray pardon him, for his falseness, I did Sir,
Both times; I'd rather be found rude, than faithless.

DUKE
I love that bluntness dearly: h'as no vice,
But is more manly than some others virtue,
That lets it out only for shew or profit.

SHAMOUNT
Will't please you quit me, Sir, I've urgent business?

DUKE
Come, you're so hasty now, I sent for you
To a better end.

SHAMOUNT
And if it be an end,
Better or worse, I thank your goodness for't.

DUKE

I've ever kept that bounty in condition,
And thankfulness in bloud, which well becomes
Both Prince and Subject, that where any wrong
Bears my impression, or the hasty figure
Of my repented anger, I'm a Law
Ev'n to my self, and doom my self most strictly
To Justice, and a noble satisfaction:
So that, what you, in tenderness of honor,
Conceive to be loss to you, which is nothing
But curious opinion, I'll restore agen,
Although I give you the best part of Genoa,
And take to boot but thanks for your amends.

SHAMOUNT
Oh miserable satisfaction,
Ten times more wretched than the wrong it self;
Never was ill better made good with worse:
Shall it be said, that my posterity
Shall live the sole heires of their fathers shame?
And raise their wealth and glory from my stripes?
You have provided nobly, bounteous Sir,
For my disgrace, to make it live for ever,
Out-lasting Brass or Marble:
This is my fears construction, and a deep one,
Which neither argument nor time can alter:
Yet I dare swear, I wrong your goodness in't Sir,
And the most fair intent on't, which I reverence
With admiration, that in you a Prince,
Should be so sweet and temperate a condition,
To offer to restore where you may ruine,
And do't with justice, and in me a servant,
So harsh a disposition, that I cannot
Forgive where I should honor, and am bound to't.
But I have ever had that curiosity
In bloud, and tenderness of reputation
Such an antipathy against a blow,
I cannot speak the rest: Good Sir discharge me,
It is not fit that I should serve you more,
Nor come so near you; I'm made now for privacy,
And a retir'd condition, that's my suit:
To part from Court for ever, my last suit;
And as you profess bounty, grant me that Sir.

DUKE
I would deny thee nothing.

SHAMOUNT
Health reward you, Sir.

[Exit.

DUKE
He's gone agen already, and takes hold
Of any opportunity: not riches
Can purchase him, nor honors, peaceably,
And force were brutish: what a great worth's gone with him,
And but a Gentleman? well, for his sake,
I'll ne'er offend more, those I cannot make;
They were his words, and shall be dear to memory.
Say I desire to see him once agen;
Yet stay, he's so well forward of his peace,
'Twere pity to disturb him: he would groan
Like a soul fetch'd agen; and that were injury,
And I've wrong'd his degree too much already.
Call forth the Gentlemen of our chamber instantly.

FIRST SERVANT
I shall my Lord.

[Within.

DUKE
I may forget agen,
And therefore will prevent: the strain of this
Troubles me so, one would not hazard more.

[Enter **FIRST GENTLEMAN**.

FIRST GENTLEMEN
Your Will my Lord?

DUKE
Yes; I discharge you all.

SECOND GENTLEMEN
My Lord—

DUKE
Your places shall be otherwise dispos'd of.

FOURTH GENTLEMEN
Why Sir?

DUKE
Reply not, I dismiss you all:
Y'are Gentlemen, your worths will find you fortunes;

Nor shall your farewell taxe me of ingratitude.
I'll give you all noble remembrances,
As testimonies 'gainst reproach and malice,
That you departed lov'd.

THIRD GENTLEMEN
This is most strange, Sir.

FIRST GENTLEMEN
But how is your Grace furnish'd, these dismiss'd?

DUKE
Seek me out Grooms.
Men more insensible of reputation,
Less curious and precise in terms of honor,
That if my anger chance let fall a stroke,
As we are all subject to impetuous passions,
Yet it may pass unmurmur'd, undisputed;
And not with braver fury prosecuted.

[Exit.

FIRST GENTLEMEN
It shall be done, my Lord.

THIRD GENTLEMEN
Know you the cause, Sir?

FIRST GENTLEMEN
Not I kind Gentlemen, but by conjectures,
And so much shall be yours when you please.

FOURTH GENTLEMEN
Thanks Sir.

THIRD GENTLEMEN
We shall i'th mean time think our selves guilty
Of some foul fault, through ignorance committed.

FIRST GENTLEMEN
No, 'tis not that, nor that way.

FOURTH GENTLEMEN
For my part,
I shall be dis-inherited, I know so much.

FIRST GENTLEMEN
Why Sir, for what?

FOURTH GENTLEMEN
My Sire's of a strange humor,
He'll form faults for me, and then swear 'em mine,
And commonly the first begins with leachery,
He knows his own youths trespass.

FIRST GENTLEMEN
Before you go,
I'll come and take my leave, and tell you all Sirs.

THIRD GENTLEMEN
Thou wert ever just and kind.

[Exit.

FIRST GENTLEMEN
That's my poor virtue, Sir,
And parcel valiant; but it's hard to be perfect:
The choosing of these fellows now will puzle me,
Horribly puzle me; and there's no judgement
Goes true upon mans outside, there's the mischief:
He must be touch'd, and try'd, for gold or dross;
There is no other way for't, and that's dangerous too;
But since I'm put in trust, I will attempt it:
The Duke shall keep one daring man about him.

[Enter **A GALLANT**

Soft, who comes here? a pretty bravery this:
Every one goes so like a Gentleman,
'Tis hard to find a difference, but by th' touch.
I'll try your mettal sure.

GALLANT
Why what do you mean Sir?

FIRST GENTLEMEN
Nay, and you understand it not, I do not.

GALLANT
Yes, would you should well know,
I understand it for a box o'th' ear Sir.

FIRST GENTLEMEN
And o'my troth, that's all I gave it for.

GALLANT

'Twere best it be so.

FIRST GENTLEMEN
This is a brave Coward,
A jolly threat'ning Coward; he shall be Captain:
Sir, let me meet you an hour hence i'th' Lobby.

GALLANT
Meet you? the world might laugh at me then i'faith.

FIRST GENTLEMEN
Lay by your scorn and pride, they're scurvy qualities,
And meet me, or I'll box you while I have you,
And carry you gambril'd thither like a Mutton.

GALLANT
Nay, and you be in earnest, here's my hand.
I will not fail you.

FIRST GENTLEMEN
'Tis for your own good.

GALLANT
Away.

FIRST GENTLEMEN
Too much for your own good, Sir, a pox on you.

GALLANT
I prethee curse me all day long so.

FIRST GENTLEMEN
Hang you.

GALLANT
I'll make him mad: he's loth to curse too much to me;
Indeed I never yet took box o'th' ear,
But it redounded, I must needs say so—

FIRST GENTLEMEN
Will you be gone?

GALLANT
Curse, curse, and then I goe.
Look how he grins, I've anger'd him to th' kidneys.

[Exit.

FIRST GENTLEMEN
Was ever such a prigging coxcomb seen?
One might have beat him dumb now in this humor,
And he'd ha' grin'd it out still:

[Enter a **PLAIN FELLOW**.

Oh, here's one made to my hand,
Methinks looks like a Craven;
Less pains will serve his trial: some slight justle.

PLAIN FELLOW
How? take you that Sir:
And if that content you not—

FIRST GENTLEMEN
Yes very well, Sir, I desire no more.

PLAIN FELLOW
I think you need not;
For you have not lost by't.

[Exit.

FIRST GENTLEMEN
Who would ha' thought this would have prov'd a Gentleman?
I'll never trust long chins and little legs agen,
I'll know 'em sure for Gentlemen hereafter:
A gristle but in shew, but gave his cuff
With such a fetch, and reach of gentry,
As if h' had had his arms before the floud;
I have took a villanous hard taske upon me;
Now I begin to have a feeling on't.

[Enter **LAPET AND CLOWN**

Oh, here comes a try'd piece, now, the reformed kick.
The millions of punches, spurns, and nips
That he has endur'd! his buttock's all black Lead,
He's half a Negro backward; he was past a Spaniard
In Eighty eight, and more Ægyptian like;
His Table and his Book come both out shortly,
And all the cowards in the Town expect it;
So, if I fail of my full number now,
I shall be sure to find 'em at Church corners,
Where Dives, and the suff'ring Ballads hang.

LAPET

Well, since thou art of so mild a temper,
Of so meek a spirit, thou mayst live with me,
Till better times do smile on thy deserts.
I am glad I am got home again.

CLOWN
I am happy in your service, Sir,
You'll keep me from the Hospital.

LAPET
So, bring me the last proof, this is corrected.

CLOWN
I, y'are too full of your correction, Sir.

LAPET
Look I have perfect Books within this half hour.

CLOWN
Yes Sir.

LAPET
Bid him put all the Thumps in Pica Roman.
And with great T's, (you vermin) as Thumps should be.

CLOWN
Then in what Letter will you have your Kicks?

LAPET
All in Italica, your backward blows
All in Italica, you Hermaphrodite:
When shall I teach you wit?

CLOWN
Oh let it alone,
Till you have some your self, Sir.

LAPET
You mumble?

CLOWN
The victuals are lockt up;
I'm kept from mumbling.

[Exit.

LAPET
He prints my blows upon Pot Paper too, the rogue,

Which had been proper for some drunken Pamphlet.

FIRST GENTLEMEN
Monsieur Lapet? how the world rings of you, Sir!
Your name sounds far and near.

LAPET
A good report it bears, for an enduring name—

FIRST GENTLEMEN
What luck have you Sir?

LAPET
Why, what's the matter?

FIRST GENTLEMEN
I'm but thinking on't.
I've heard you wish these five years for a place.
Now there's one fall'n, and freely without money too;
And empty yet, and yet you cannot have't.

LAPET
No? what's the reason? I'll give money for't,
Rather than go without Sir.

FIRST GENTLEMEN
That's not it Sir:
The troth is, there's no Gentleman must have it
Either for love or money, 'tis decreed so;
I was heartily sorry when I thought upon you,
Had you not been a Gentleman, I had fitted you.

LAPET
Who I a Gentleman? a pox I'm none, Sir.

FIRST GENTLEMEN
How?

LAPET
How? why did you ever think I was?

FIRST GENTLEMEN
What? not a Gentleman?

LAPET
I would thou'dst put it upon me i'faith;
Did not my Grand-father cry Cony-skins?
My Father Aquavitæ? a hot Gentleman:

All this I speak on, i' your time and memory too;
Only a rich Uncle dy'd, and left me chattels,
You know all this so well too—

FIRST GENTLEMEN
Pray excuse me, Sir, ha' not you Arms?

LAPET
Yes, a poor couple here,
That serve to thrust in wild-Fowl.

FIRST GENTLEMEN
Heralds Arms,
Symbols of Gentry, Sir: you know my meaning;
They've been shewn and seen.

LAPET
They have.

FIRST GENTLEMEN
I fex have they.

LAPET
Why I confess, at my wives instigation once,
(As Women love these Heralds kickshawes naturally)
I bought 'em: but what are they think you? puffs.

FIRST GENTLEMEN
Why, that's proper to your name being Lapet.
Which is La fart, after the English Letter.

LAPET
The Herald, Sir, had much adoe to find it.

FIRST GENTLEMEN
And can you blame him?
Why, 'tis the only thing that puzles the devil.

LAPET
At last he lookt upon my name agen,
And having well compar'd it, this he gave me,
The two Cholliques playing upon a wind Instrument.

FIRST GENTLEMEN
An excellent proper one; but I pray tell me,
How does he express the Cholliques?
They are hard things.

LAPET

The Cholliques? with hot trenchers at their bellies;
There's nothing better, Sir, to blaze a Chollique.

FIRST GENTLEMEN

And are not you a Gentleman by this Sir?

LAPET

No, I disclaim't: no belly-ake upon earth
Shall make me one: he shall not think
To put his gripes upon me,
And wring out gentry so, and ten pound first.
If the wind Instrument will make my wife one,
Let her enjoy't, for she was a Harpers Grand-child:
But Sir, for my particular, I renounce it.

FIRST GENTLEMEN

Or to be call'd so?

LAPET

I Sir, or imagin'd.

FIRST GENTLEMEN

None fitter for the place: give me thy hand.

LAPET

A hundred thousand thanks, beside a Bribe, Sir.

FIRST GENTLEMEN

You must take heed
Of thinking toward a Gentleman, now.

LAPET

Pish, I am not mad, I warrant you: nay, more Sir,
If one should twit me i'th' teeth that I'm a Gentleman,
Twit me their worst, I am but one since Lammas,
That I can prove, if they would see my heart out.

FIRST GENTLEMEN

Marry, in any case keep me that evidence.

[Enter **CLOWN**

LAPET

Here comes my Servant; Sir, Galoshio,
Has not his name for nought, he will be trode upon:
What says my Printer now?

CLOWN

Here's your last Proof, Sir.

You shall have perfect Books now in a twinkling.

LAPET

These marks are ugly.

CLOWN

He says, Sir, they're proper:

Blows should have marks, or else they are nothing worth.

LADY

But why a Peel-crow here?

CLOWN

I told 'em so Sir:

A scare-crow had been better.

LAPET

How slave? look you, Sir,

Did not I say, this Whirrit, and this Bob,

Should be both Pica Roman.

CLOWN

So said I, Sir, both Picked Romans,

And he has made 'em Welch Bills,

Indeed I know not what to make on 'em.

LAPET

Hay-day; a Souse, Italica?

CLOWN

Yes, that may hold, Sir,

Souse is a bona roba, so is Flops too.

LAPET

But why stands Bastinado so far off here?

CLOWN

Alas, you must allow him room to lay about him, Sir.

LADY

Why lies this Spurn lower than that Spurn, Sir?

CLOWN

Marry, this signifies one kickt down stairs, Sir,

The other in a Gallery: I asked him all these questions.

FIRST GENTLEMEN
Your Books name?
Prethee Lapet mind me, you never told me yet.

LADY
Marry but shall Sir: 'tis call'd the Uprising of the kick;
And the downfall of the Duello.

FIRST GENTLEMEN
Bring that to pass, you'll prove a happy member,
And do your Countrey service: your young blouds
Will thank you then, why they see fourscore.

LAPET
I hope
To save my hundred Gentlemen a month by't,
Which will be very good for the private house.

CLOWN
Look you, your Table's finish'd, Sir, already.

LAPET
Why then behold my Master-piece: see, see, Sir,
Here's all your Blows, and Blow-men whatsoever;
Set in their lively colours, givers, and takers.

FIRST GENTLEMEN
Troth wondrous fine, Sir.

LAPET
Nay, but mark the postures,
The standing of the takers, I admire more than the givers;
They stand scornfully, most contumeliously, I like not them,
Oh here's one cast into a comely Figure.

CLOWN
My Master means him there that's cast down headlong.

LAPET
How sweetly does this fellow take his Dowst!
Stoops like a Cammel, that Heroick beast,
At a great load of Nutmegs; and how meekly
This other fellow here receives his Whirrit!

CLOWN
Oh Master, here's a fellow stands most gallantly,
Taking his kick in private, behind the hangings,
And raising up his hips to't. But oh, Sir,

How daintily this man lies trampled on!
Would I were in thy place, what e'er thou art:
How lovely he endures it!

FIRST GENTLEMEN
But will not these things, Sir, be hard to practice, think
you?

LAPET
Oh, easie, Sir: I'll teach 'em in a Dance.

FIRST GENTLEMEN
How? in a dance?

LAPET
I'll lose my new place else,
What e'er it be; I know not what 'tis yet.

FIRST GENTLEMEN
And now you put me in mind, I could employ it well,
For your grace, specially: For the Dukes Cosin
Is by this time in's violent fit of mirth,
And a device must be sought out for suddainly,
To over-cloy the passion.

LAPET
Say no more, Sir,
I'll fit you with my Scholars, new practitioners,
Endurers of the time.

CLOWN
Whereof I am one Sir.

FIRST GENTLEMEN
You carry it away smooth; give me thy hand, Sir. Exeunt.

ACTUS QUINTUS

SCÆNA PRIMA

[Enter the **TWO BROTHERS**

PASSIONATE LORD
Ha, ha, ha.

[Within.

SECOND BROTHER
Hark, hark, how loud his fit's grown.

PASSIONATE LORD
Ha, ha, ha.

FIRST BROTHER
Now let our Sister lose no time, but ply it
With all the power she has.

SECOND BROTHER
Her shame grows big, brother;
The Cupid's shape will hardly hold it longer,
'Twould take up half an Ell of China Damask more,
And all too little: it struts per'lously:
There is no tamp'ring with these Cupids longer,
The meer conceit with Woman-kind works strong.

PASSIONATE LORD
Ha, ha, ha.

SECOND BROTHER
The laugh comes nearer now,
'Twere good we were not seen yet.

[Exit **BROTHERS**.

[Enter **PASSION, AND BASE**

PASSIONATE LORD
Ha, ha, ha,
And was he bastinado'd to the life? ha, ha, ha.
I prethee say, Lord General, how did the rascals
Entrench themselves?

BASE
Most deeply, politickly, all in ditches.

PASSIONATE LORD
Ha, ha, ha.

BASE
'Tis thought he'll ne'r bear Arms ith' field agen,
Has much ado to lift 'em to his head, Sir.

PASSIONATE LORD
I would he had.

BASE
On either side round Truncheons plaid so thick,
That Shoulders, Chines, nay Flanks were paid to th' quick.

PASSIONATE LORD
Well said Lord-General: ha, ha, ha.

BASE
But pray how grew the diff'rence first betwixt you?

PASSIONATE LORD
There was never any, Sir; there lies the jest man;
Only because he was taller than his brother;
There's all my quarrel, to him; and methought
He should be beaten for't, my mind so gave me, Sir,
I could not sleep for't: Ha, ha, ha, ha.
Another good jest quickly, while 'tis hot now;
Let me not laugh in vain: ply me, oh ply me,
As you will answer't to my cosin Duke.

BASE
Alas, who has a good jest?

PASSIONATE LORD
I fall, I dwindle in't.

BASE
Ten Crowns for a good jest: ha' you a good jest, Sir?

[Enter **SERVANT**.

SERVANT
A pretty moral one.

BASE
Let's ha't, what e'er it be.

SERVANT
There comes a Cupid
Drawn by six fools.

BASE
That's nothing.

PASSIONATE LORD
Help it, help it then.

BASE
I ha' known six hundred fools drawn by a Cupid.

PASSIONATE LORD
I that, that, that's the smarter Moral: ha, ha, ha.
Now I begin to be Song-ripe methinks.

BASE
I'll sing you a pleasant Air Sir, before you ebb.

[SONG

PASSIONATE LORD
Oh how my Lungs do tickle! ha, ha, ha.

BASE
Oh how my Lungs do tickle! oh, oh, ho, ho.

PASSIONATE LORD [Sings]
Set a sharp Jest
Against my breast,
Then how my Lungs do tickle!
As Nightingales,
And things in Cambrick rails,
Sing best against a prickle,
Ha, ha, ha, ha.

BASE
Ho, ho, ho, ho, ha.

PASSIONATE LORD
Laugh.

BASE
Laugh.

PASSIONATE LORD
Laugh.

BASE
Laugh.

PASSIONATE LORD
Wide.

BASE
Loud.

PASSIONATE LORD
And vary.

BASE
A smile is for a simpering Novice.

PASSIONATE LORD
One that ne'er tasted Caveare.

BASE
Nor knows the smack of dear Anchovis.

PASSIONATE LORD
Ha, ha, ha, ha, ha.

BASE
Ho, ho, ho, ho, ho.

PASSIONATE LORD
A gigling waiting wench for me,
That shews her teeth how white they be.

BASE
A thing not fit for gravity,
For theirs are foul, and hardly three.

PASSIONATE LORD
Ha, ha, ha.

BASE
Ho, ho, ho.

PASSIONATE LORD
Democritus, thou antient Fleerer,
How I miss thy laugh, and ha' since.

BASE
There you nam'd the famous Jeerer,
That ever jeer'd in Rome, or Athens.

PASSIONATE LORD
Ha, ha, ha.

BASE
Ho, ho, ho.

PASSIONATE LORD
How brave lives he that keeps a fool,

Although the rate be deeper!

BASE
But he that is his own fool, Sir,
Does live a great deal cheaper.

PASSIONATE LORD
Sure I shall burst, burst, quite break, thou art so witty.

BASE
'Tis rare to break at Court, for that belongs to th' City.

PASSIONATE LORD
Ha, ha, my spleen is almost worn to the last laughter.

BASE
Oh keep a corner for a friend, a jest may come hereafter.

LAPET
Twinge all now, twinge I say.
2 Strain.
Souse upon Souse.
3 Strain.
Douses single.
4 Strain.
Justle sides.
5 Strain.
Knee Belly.
6 Strain.
Kicksee Buttock.
7 Strain.

LADY
Downderry.

[Enter **SOLDIER, SHAMOUNT'S BROTHER**

SOLDIER
Not angry Law, nor doors of Brass shall keep me,
From my wrongs expiation to thy Bowels,
I return my disgrace; and after turn
My face to any death that can be sentenc'd.

BASE
Murder, oh murder, stop the murderer there—

LAPET
I am glad he's gone; h'as almost trode my guts out;

Follow him who list for me, I'll ha' no hand in't.

CLOWN
Oh 'twas your luck and mine to be squelch'd, Mr.
H'as stamp'd my very Puddings into Pancakes.

CUPID
Oh brothers, oh, I fear 'tis mortal: help, oh help,
I'm made the wretchedst woman by this accident,
That ever love beguil'd.

[Enter **TWO BROTHERS.**

SECOND BROTHER
We are undone Brother,
Our shames are too apparent: Away receptacle
Of Luxury, and dishonor, most unfortunate,
To make thy self but lucky to thy spoil,
After thy Sexes manner: lift him up Brother;
He breaths not to our comfort, he's too wasted
Ever to cheer us more: A Chirurgeon speedily;
Hence; the unhappiest that e'er stept aside,
She'll be a Mother, before she's known a Bride.

CUPID
Thou hadst a most unfortunate conception,
What e'er thou prov'st to be; in midst of mirth
Comes ruine, for a welcome, to thy birth.

[Exeunt.

SCÆNA SECUNDA

[Enter **SHAMOUNT.**

SHAMOUNT
This is a beautiful life now; privacy
The sweetness and the benefit of Essence:
I see there is no man, but may make his Paradice;
And it is nothing but his love, and dotage
Upon the worlds foul joyes, that keeps him out on't:
For he that lives retir'd in mind, and spirit,
Is still in Paradice, and has his innocence,
Partly allow'd for his companion too,
As much as stands with justice: here no eyes
Shoot their sharp pointed scorns upon my shame;

They know no terms of reputation here,
No punctual limits, or precise dimensions:
Plain down-right honesty is all the beauty
And elegancy of life, found amongst Shepheards;
For knowing nothing nicely, or desiring it,
Quits many a vexation from the mind,
With which our quainter knowledge does abuse us;
The name of envy is a stranger here,
That dries mens blouds abroad, robs Health and Rest,
Why here's no such fury thought on: no, nor falshood,
That brotherly disease, fellow-like devil,
That plays within our bosom, and betrays us.

[Enter **FIRST GENTLEMEN**

FIRST GENTLEMEN
Oh are you here?

SHAMOUNT
La Nove, 'tis strange to see thee.

FIRST GENTLEMEN
I ha' rid one horse to death,
To find you out, Sir.

SHAMOUNT
I am not to be found of any man
That saw my shame, nor seen long.

FIRST GENTLEMEN
Good, your attention:
You ought to be seen now, and found out, Sir,
If ever you desire before your ending
To perform one good office, nay, a dear one,
Mans time can hardly match it.

SHAMOUNT
Be't as precious
As reputation; if it come from Court
I will not hear on't.

FIRST GENTLEMEN
You must hear of this, Sir.

SHAMOUNT
Must?

FIRST GENTLEMEN

You shall hear it.

SHAMOUNT
I love thee, that thou'lt dye.

FIRST GENTLEMEN
'Twere nobler in me,
Than in you living: you will live a murderer,
If you deny this office.

SHAMOUNT
Even to death, Sir.

FIRST GENTLEMEN
Why then you'll kill your brother.

SHAMOUNT
How?

FIRST GENTLEMEN
Your Brother, Sir:
Bear witness heaven, this man destroys his Brother
When he may save him, his least breath may save him:
Can there be wilfuller destruction?
He was forc'd to take a most unmanly wrong,
Above the suff'ring virtue of a Soldier,
Has kill'd his injurer, a work of honor;
For which, unless you save him, he dies speedily
My conscience is discharg'd, I'm but a friend,
A Brother should go forward where I end.

[Exit.

SHAMOUNT
Dyes?
Say he be naught, that's nothing to my goodness,
Which ought to shine through use, or else it loses
The glorious name 'tis known by: he's my brother;
Yet peace is above bloud: Let him go; I,
But where's the nobleness of affection then?
That must be car'd for too, or I'm imperfect,
The same bloud that stood up in wrath against him,
Now in his misery, runs all to pity;
I'd rather dye than speak one syllable
To save my self, but living as I am,
There's no avoiding on't, the worlds humanity
Expects it hourly from me: curse of fortune,
I took my leave so well too: Let him dye,

'Tis but a brother lost; so pleasingly,
And swiftly I came off, 'twere more than irksomness,
To tread that path agen; and I shall never
Depart so handsomely: but then where's posterity?
The consummation of our house and name?
I'm torn in pieces betwixt love and shame.

[Exit.

[Enter **LAPET, CLOWN, POULTROT, MOULBAZON AND OTHERS**

LAPET
Good morrow fellow Poltrot, and Moulbazon,
Good morrow fellows all.

POULTROT
Monsieur Lapet?

LAPET
Look, I've remembred you, here's books apiece for you.

MOULBAZON
Oh Sir, we dearly thank you.

LAPET
So you may:
There's two impressions gone already, Sirs.

POULTROT
What no? in so short a time?

LAPET
'Tis as I tell you, Sir.
My Kick sells gallantly, I thank my stars.

CLOWN
So does your Table; you may thank the Moon too.

LAPET
'Tis the Book sells the Table.

CLOWN
But 'tis the Bookseller
That has the money for 'em, I'm sure o' that.

LAPET

'Twill much enrich the Company of Stationers,
'Tis thought 'twill prove a lasting benefit,
Like the Wise Masters, and the Almanacks,
The hundred Novels, and the Book of Cookery,
For they begin already to engross it,
And make it a Stock-book, thinking indeed
'Twill prove too great a benefit, and help,
For one that's new set up: they know their way,
And make him Warden, e'r his beard be gray.

MOULBAZON

Is't possible such virtue should lye hid,
And in so little Paper?

LAPET

How? why there was the Carpenter,
An unknown thing; an odoriferous Pamphlet,
Yet no more Paper, by all computation,
Than Ajax Telamon would use at once,
Your Herring prov'd the like, able to buy
Another Fishers Folly, and your Pasquil
Went not below the mad-caps of that time,
And shall my elaborate Kick come behind, think you?

CLOWN

Yes, it must come behind, 'tis in Italica too,
According to your humor.

LAPET

Not in sale, Varlet.

CLOWN

In sale, Sir? it shall sail beyond 'em all I tro.

LAPET

What have you there now? oh Page 21.

CLOWN

That Page is come to his years, he should be a Serving man.

LAPET

Mark how I snap up the Duello there:
One would not use a dog so,
I must needs say; but's for the common good.

CLOWN

Nay Sir, your Commons seldom fight at sharp,
But buffet in a Warehouse.

LAPET
This will save
Many a Gentleman of good bloud from bleeding, Sirs,
I have a curse from many a Barber-Surgeon;
They'd give but too much money to call't in;
Turn to Page 45. see what you find there.

CLOWN
Oh, out upon him,
Page 45. that's an old thief indeed.

[Enter **DUKE, THE LADY AND FIRST GENTLEMEN**

LAPET
The Duke, clap down your Books; away Galoshio.

CLOWN
Indeed I am too foul to be i' th' presence,
They use to shake me off at the chamber door still.

[Exit

LADY
Good my Lord, grant my suit: let me not rise
Without the comfort on't: I have not often
Been tedious in this kind.

DUKE
Sister, you wrong your self,
And those great virtues that your Fame is made of,
To waste so much breath for a murderers life.

LADY
You cannot hate th' offence more than I do, Sir,
Nor the offender, the respect I owe
Unto his absent brother, makes me a suitor,
A most importunate Sister, make me worthy
But of this one request.

DUKE
I am deaf
To any importunacy, and sorry
For your forgetfulness; you never injur'd
Your worth so much, you ought to be rebuk'd for't:
Pursue good ways, end as you did begin,

'Tis half the guilt to speak for such a sin.

LADY
This is loves beggery right, that now is ours,
When Ladies love, and cannot shew their powers.

[Exit

DUKE
La Nove?

FIRST GENTLEMEN
My Lord.

DUKE
Are these our new Attendants?

LAPET
We are my Lord, and will endure as much
As better men, my Lord, and more I trust.

DUKE
What's he?

FIRST GENTLEMEN
My Lord, a decay'd Gentleman,
That will do any service.

DUKE
A decay'd one?

FIRST GENTLEMEN
A renounc'd one indeed: for this place only.

DUKE
We renounce him then; go, discharge him instantly.
He that disclaims his gentry for meer gains,
That man's too base to make a vassal on.

LAPET
What says the Duke?

FIRST GENTLEMEN
Faith little to your comfort, Sir,
You must be a Gentleman agen.

LAPET
How?

FIRST GENTLEMEN
There's no remedy.

LAPET
Marry, the fates forefend: ne'r while I breathe, Sir.

FIRST GENTLEMEN
The Duke will have it so, there's no resisting,
He spy'd it i' your forehead.

LAPET
My wife's doing.
She thought she should be put below her betters now,
And su'd to ha' me a Gentleman agen.

FIRST GENTLEMEN
And very likely, Sir,
Marry, I'll give you this comfort when all's done,
You'll never pass but for a scurvy one,
That's all the help you have: come shew your pace.

LAPET
The heaviest Gentleman that e'er lost place;
Bear witness, I am forc'd to't.

[Exit.

DUKE
Though you have a courser Title yet upon you,
Than those that left your places, without blame,
'Tis in your power to make your selves the same:
I cannot make you Gentlemen, that's a work
Rais'd from your own deservings, merit, manners,
And in-born virtue does it. Let your own goodness
Make you so great, my power shall make you greater;
And more t'encourage you, this I add agen,
There's many Grooms, now exact Gentlemen.

[Enter **SHAMOUNT**

SHAMOUNT
Methinks 'tis strange to me to enter here:
Is there in nature such an awful power,
To force me to this place? and make me do this?
Is mans affection stronger than his Will?
His resolution? was I not resolv'd
Never to see this place more? Do I bear

Within my breast one bloud that confounds th' other?
The bloud of Love, and Will, and the last weakest?
Had I ten Millions, I would give it all now,
I were but past it, or 'twould never come;
For I shall never do't, or not do't well,
But spoil it utterly betwixt two passions,
Yonder's the Duke himself, I will not do't now,
Had twenty lives their several sufferings in him.

[Exit.

DUKE
Who's that went out now?

POULTROT
I saw none my Lord.

DUKE
Nor you?

MOULBAZON
I saw the glimpse of one my Lord.

DUKE
What e'er it was, methought it pleas'd me strangely
And suddenly my joy was ready for't.
Did you not mark it better?

POULTROT & **MOULBAZON**
Troth my Lord,
We gave no great heed to't.

[Enter **SHAMONT**.

SHAMOUNT
'Twill not be answer'd,
It brings me hither still; by main force hither:
Either I must give over to profess humanity,
Or I must speak for him.

DUKE
'Tis here agen:
No marvel 'twas so pleasing, 'tis delight
And worth it self, now it appears unclouded.

SHAMOUNT
My Lord—
He turns away from me: by this hand

I am ill-us'd of all sides: 'tis a fault
That fortune ever had t'abuse a goodness.

DUKE
Methought you were saying somewhat.

SHAMOUNT
Mark the Language,
As coy as fate; I see 'twill ne'er be granted.

DUKE
We little look'd in troth to see you here yet.

SHAMOUNT
Not till the day after my brother's death, I think.

DUKE
Sure some great business drew you.

SHAMOUNT
No insooth, Sir,
Only to come to see a brother dye, Sir,
That I may learn to go too; and if he deceive me not,
I think he will do well in't of a soldier,
Manly, and honestly: and if he weep then,
I shall not think the worse on's manhood for't,
Because he's leaving of that part that has it.

DUKE
Has slain a noble Gentleman, think on't, Sir.

SHAMOUNT
I would I could not, Sir.

DUKE
Our kinsman too.

SHAMOUNT
All this is but worse, Sir.

DUKE
When 'tis at worst,
Yet seeing thee, he lives.

SHAMOUNT
My Lord—

DUKE

He lives,
Believe it as thy bliss, he dies not for't:
Will this make satisfaction for things past?

SHAMOUNT
Oh my Lord—

DUKE
Will it? speak.

SHAMOUNT
With greater shame to my unworthiness.

DUKE
Rise then, we're even: I never found it harder
To keep just with a man: my great work's ended.
I knew your brother's pardon was your suit, Sir.
How ever your nice modesty held it back.

SHAMOUNT
I take a joy now, to confess it, Sir.

[Enter **FIRST GENTLEMEN**.

FIRST GENTLEMEN
My Lord—

DUKE
Hear me first, Sir, what e'er your news be:
Set free the Soldier instantly.

FIRST GENTLEMEN
'Tis done, my Lord.

DUKE
How?

FIRST GENTLEMEN
In effect: 'twas part of my news too,
There's fair hope of your noble kinsman's life, Sir.

DUKE
What sayst thou?

FIRST GENTLEMEN
And the most admired change
That living flesh e'r had; he's not the man my Lord;
Death cannot be more free from passions, Sir,

Than he is at this instant: he's so meek now,
He makes those seem passionate, was never thought of:
And for he fears his moods have oft disturb'd you, Sir,
He's only hasty now for his forgiveness,
And here behold him, Sir.

[Enter **PASSIONATE LORD**, the **CUPID**, and **TWO BROTHERS**.

DUKE
Let me give thanks first: our worthy Cosin—

PASSIONATE LORD
Your unworthy trouble, Sir;
For which, with all acknowledg'd reverence,
I ask your pardon; and for injury
More known and wilful, I have chose a wife,
Without your counsel, or consent, my Lord.

DUKE
A wife? where is she, Sir?

PASSIONATE LORD
This noble Gentlewoman.

DUKE
How?

PASSIONATE LORD
Whose honor my forgetful times much wrong'd.

DUKE
He's madder than he was.

FIRST GENTLEMEN
I would ha' sworn for him.

DUKE
The Cupid, Cosin?

PASSIONATE LORD
Yes, this worthy Lady, Sir.

DUKE
Still worse and worse.

FIRST BROTHER
Our Sister under pardon, my Lord.

DUKE
What?

SECOND BROTHER
Which shape Love taught her to assume.

DUKE
Is't truth then?

FIRST GENTLEMEN
It appears plainly now, below the waste, my Lord.

DUKE
Shamont, didst ever read of a She-Cupid?

SHAMOUNT
Never in fiction yet: but it might hold, Sir;
For desire is of both Genders.

[Enter the **DUKE'S SISTER**.

DUKE
Make that good here:
He joyns Shamont's hand
I take thee at thy word,
Sir and his Sisters.

SHAMOUNT
Oh my Lord,
Love would appear too bold, and rude from me,
Honour and admiration are her rights,
Her goodness is my Saint, my Lord.

DUKE
I see,
Y'are both too modest to bestow your selves:
I'll save that virtue still, 'tis but my pains: come,
It shall be so.

SHAMOUNT
This gift does but set forth my poverty.

LADY
Sir, that which you complain of, is my riches.

[Enter Shamount's Brother the **SOLDIER**

DUKE

Soldier, now every noise sounds peace, th'art welcome.

SOLDIER
Sir, my repentance sues for your blest favour,
Which once obtain'd, no injury shall lose it;
I'll suffer mightier wrongs.

DUKE
Rise, lov'd and pardon'd:
For where Hope fail'd, nay Art it self resign'd,
Thou'st wrought that cure, which skill could never find;
Nor did there cease, but to our peace extend;
Never could wrongs boast of a nobler end.

[Exeunt.

EPILOGUE

Our Poet bid us say for his own part,
He cannot lay too much forth of his Art:
But fears our over-acting passions may,
As not adorn, deface his labour'd Play,
Yet still he's resolute, for what is writ
Of Nicer valour, and assumes the wit:
But for the Love-Scænes which he ever meant,
Cupid in's Peticoat should represent,
He'll stand no shock of censure; the Play's good,
He says he knows it, (if well understood.)
But we (blind god) beg, if thou art Divine,
Thou'lt shoot thy Arrows round, this Play was thine.

Mr. Francis Beaumonts Letter to Ben. Johnson, written before he and Mr. Fletcher came to London, with two of the precedent Comedies then not finish'd, which deferr'd their merry meetings at the Mermaid.

The Sun which doth the greatest comfort bring
To absent friends, because the self-same thing
They know they see however absent, is,
Here our best Hay-maker forgive me this,
It is our Countreys stile. In this warm shine,
I lye and dream of your full Mermaid Wine.
Oh we have water mixt with Claret Lees,
Drink apt to bring in dryer Heresies
Than Beer, good only for the Sonnets strain,
With fustian Metaphors to stuff the brain,
So mixt, that given to the thirstiest one,

'Twill not prove Alms, unless he have the stone:
I think with one draught mans invention fades,
Two Cups had quite spoil'd Homers Illiads;
'Tis Liquor that will find out Sutcliff's wit,
Lye where he will, and make him write worse yet;
Fil'd with such moisture in most grievous qualms;
Did Robert Wisdom write his Singing Psalms;
And so must I do this, and yet I think
It is a potion sent us down to drink,
By special Providence keeps us from fights,
Makes us not laugh, when we make legs to knights.
'Tis this that keeps our minds fit for our States,
A Medicine to obey our Magistrates:
For we do live more free than you, no hate,
No envy at one anothers happy State
Moves us, we are all equal every whit:
Of Land that God gives men here is their wit:
If we consider fully, for our best,
And gravest men will with his main house jest,
Scarce please you; we want subtilty to do
The City tricks, lye, hate, and flatter too:
Here are none that can bear a painted show,
Strike when you winch, and then lament the blow:
Who like Mills set the right way for to grind,
Can make their gains alike with every wind:
Only some fellows with the subtil'st pate
Amongst us, may perchance equivocate
At selling of a Horse, and that's the most.
Methinks the little wit I had is lost
Since I saw you, for Wit is like a Rest
Held up at Tennis, which men do the best,
With the best gamesters: what things have we seen,
Done at the Mermaid! heard words that have been
So nimble, and so full of subtil flame,
As if that every one from whence they came,
Had meant to put his whole wit in a jest,
And had resolv'd to live a fool, the rest
Of his dull life; then when there hath been thrown
Wit able enough to justifie the Town
For three days past, wit that might warrant be
For the whole City to talk foolishly
Till that were cancell'd, and when that was gone,
We left an Air behind us, which alone,
Was able to make the two next Companies
Right witty; though but downright fools, more wise.
When I remember this, and see that now
The Countrey Gentlemen begin to allow
My wit for dry bobs, then I needs must cry,

I see my days of Ballating grow nigh;
I can already Riddle, and can Sing
Catches, sell bargains, and I fear shall bring
My self to speak the hardest words I find,
Over, as oft as any, with one wind,
That takes no medicines: But one thought of thee
Makes me remember all these things to be
The wit of our young men, fellows that show
No part of good, yet utter all they know:
Who like trees of the Guard, have growing souls.
Only strong destiny, which all controuls,
I hope hath left a better fate in store,
For me thy friend, than to live ever poor,
Banisht unto this home; fate once again
Bring me to thee, who canst make smooth and plain
The way of Knowledge for me, and then I,
Who have no good but in thy company,
Protest it will my greatest comfort be
To acknowledge all I have to flow from thee.

Ben. when these Scænes are perfect, we'll taste wine;
I'll drink thy Muses health, thou shalt quaff mine.

Thomas Middleton – A Short Biography

Thomas Middleton was born in London in April 1580 and baptised on 18th April. He was the son of a bricklayer who had raised himself to the status of a gentleman and become the owner of property adjoining the Curtain Theatre in Shoreditch.

Middleton was aged only five when his father died. His mother remarried but this new union unfortunately fell apart and turned into a fifteen year legal conflict centered on the inheritance of Thomas and his younger sister.

Middleton went on to attend Queen's College, Oxford, matriculating in 1598. However he failed to graduate for reasons unknown leaving either in 1600 or 1601. He had by that time written and published three long poems in popular Elizabethan styles. None appears to have been commercially successful although Microcynicon: Six Snarling Satirese was denounced by the Archbishop of Canterbury and publicly burned as part of his attack on verse satire. Although a minor work, the poems show the roots of Middleton's interest in, and later mature work on, sin, hypocrisy, and lust.

In the early years of the 17th century, Middleton made a living writing topical pamphlets, including one, Penniless Parliament of Threadbare Poets, that was reprinted several times as well as becoming the subject of a parliamentary inquiry.

For one so young he was already making quite an impact and had obviously attracted the eye of the authorities in those turbulent times.

Records surviving of the great theatrical entrepreneur of the day, Philip Henslowe, confirm that Middleton was writing for Henslowe's Admiral's Men. His lauded contemporary, a certain William Shakespeare, was writing only for Henslowe whereas Middleton remained a free agent and able to write for whichever theatrical company hired him.

These early years writing plays continued to attract controversy. His friendship and writing partnership with Thomas Dekker brought him into conflict with Ben Jonson and George Chapman in the so-called War of the Theatres. (This controversy was also called the Poetomachia by Thomas Dekker. The Bishops Ban of 1599 had removed any use of satire from prose and verse publications and so the only outlet was on the stage. For the next 3 years Ben Jonson and George Chapman on one side and John Marston, Thomas Dekker and Thomas Middleton on the other poked fun at their opposition with characters from their plays. The grudge against Jonson continued as late as 1626, when Jonson's play The Staple of News indulges in a slur on Middleton's last play, A Game at Chess).

In 1603, Middleton married. It was also a momentous year in other respects. On the death of Elizabeth I, her cousin James VI of Scotland was now also crowned King James I of England. Another outbreak of the plague now forced the theatres in London to close.

For Middleton the changeover from Elizabethan to Jacobean was the beginning of a long period of success as a writer.

When the theatres re-opened and welcomed back audiences in need of entertainment Middleton was there, writing for several different companies. In particular he specialised in city comedy and revenge tragedy.

During this time he appears also to have written with Shakespeare and he is variously attributed as collaborating on All's Well That Ends Well and Timon of Athens.

Although Middleton had started as a junior partner to Thomas Dekker he was now his fully fledged equal. His finest work with Dekker was undoubtedly The Roaring Girl, a biography of the notorious contemporary thief Mary Frith (Frith began her criminal career as a pickpocket before moving on to highway robbery with a penchant for dressing up as a man. A spell in prison was followed by a long career as a 'fence' from her shop in Fleet St. She lived to the then quite extraordinary age of 74.) The writing is noteworthy not only for its playwriting ambition but in producing a fully formed heroine in Moll Cutpurse. This was only shortly after the role of women in plays had seen fit to have them played, in the main, by men.

In the 1610s, Middleton began another playwriting partnership, this time with the actor William Rowley, producing another slew of plays including the classics Wit at Several Weapons and A Fair Quarrel.

The ever adaptable Middleton seemed at ease working with others or by himself. His solo writing credits include the comic masterpiece, A Chaste Maid in Cheapside, in 1613. Interestingly his solo plays are somewhat less thrusting and bellicose. Certainly there is no comedy among them with the satirical depth of Michaelmas Term and no tragedy as raw, striking and as bloodthirsty as The Revenger's Tragedy.

There may be various reasons for this and among them that he was increasingly involved with civic pageants and therefore was trying to avoid too much controversy especially without the cover of a collaborator. Indeed in 1620, he was officially appointed as chronologer of the City of London, a post he held until his death in 1627, when ironically, it passed to his great rival, and sometime enemy, Ben Jonson.

Middleton's official duties did not interrupt his dramatic writing; the 1620s saw the production of his and Rowley's tragedy, and continual favourite, The Changeling, as well as several other tragicomedies.

However in 1624, he reached a peak of notoriety when his dramatic allegory A Game at Chess was staged by the King's Men. The play used the conceit of a chess game to present and satirise the recent intrigues surrounding the Spanish Match; James I's son, Prince Charles, was being positioned to marry the daughter, Maria Anna of the Spanish King Philip IV of Spain. Though Middleton's approach was strongly patriotic, the Privy Council closed the play, after only nine performances at the Globe theatre, having received a complaint from the Spanish ambassador. The Privy Council then opened a prosecution against both authors and actors. Although Middleton in his defence showed that the play had been passed by the Master of the Revels, Sir Henry Herbert, any further performance was forbidden and the author and actors fined.

What happened next is a mystery. It is the last play recorded as having being written by Middleton. His playwriting career appears to have stopped dead. It follows that some sort of further punishment probably occurred and for a writer can there be any greater punishment than not being allowed to write or be heard?

Middleton's work is diverse even by the standards of his age. His career Middleton covers many many genres including tragedy, history and city comedy. As we have noted he did not have the kind of official relationship with a particular company that Shakespeare or Fletcher had that might have supported him in a lean creative period. Instead he appears to have written on a freelance basis for any number of companies. His output ranges from the "snarling" satire of Michaelmas Term, performed by the Children of Paul's, to the bleak intrigues of The Revenger's Tragedy, performed by the King's Men. Interestingly earlier editions of The Revenger's Tragedy attributed the play solely to Cyril Tourneur but recent studies have shredded that view so that Middleton's authorship is not now seriously contested

Indeed modern techniques in analysing writing styles are now leaning towards giving Middleton credit for his adaptation and revision of Shakespeare's Macbeth and Measure for Measure. Along with the more established evidence of collaboration on All's Well That Ends Well and Timon of Athens it appears that Middleton has moved some way forward to the front rank of playwrights and an association, in some form, but its greatest exponent.

His early work was informed by the blossoming, in the late Elizabethan period, of satire, while his maturity was influenced by the ascendancy of Fletcherian tragicomedy. Middleton's later work, in which his satirical fury is tempered and broadened, includes three of his acknowledged masterpieces. A Chaste Maid in Cheapside, produced by the Lady Elizabeth's Men, which skillfully combines London life with an expansive view of the power of love to effect reconciliation even though London seems populated entirely by sinners, in which no social rank goes unsatirised. The Changeling, a later tragedy, returns Middleton to an Italianate setting like that of The Revenger's Tragedy, except that here the central characters are more fully drawn and more compelling as individuals. Similar development can be seen in Women Beware Women.

Middleton's plays are marked by their cynicism, though often very funny, about the human race. His characters are complex. True heroes are a rarity: almost all of his characters are selfish, greedy, and self-absorbed.

When Middleton does portray good people, the characters are often presented as flawless and perfect and given small, undemanding roles. A theological pamphlet attributed to Middleton gives sustenance to the notion that Middleton was a strong believer in Calvinism.

Thomas Middleton died at his home at Newington Butts in Southwark in the summer of 1627, and was buried on July 4th, in St Mary's churchyard which today survives as a public park in Elephant and Castle.

Middleton stands with John Fletcher and Ben Jonson as the most successful and prolific of playwrights from the Jacobean period. Very few Renaissance dramatists would achieve equal success in both comedy and tragedy but Middleton was one. He also wrote many masques and pageants and remains, to this day, one of the most notable of Jacobean dramatists.

Middleton's work has long been praised by many literary critics, among the most fervent were Algernon Charles Swinburne and T. S. Eliot. The latter thought Middleton was second only to Shakespeare.

Among their contemporaries was a very crowded field of talent including: Ben Jonson (1572-1637), Christopher Marlowe (1564-1593), Francis Beaumont (1585-1616), Henry Chettle (1564-1606), John Fletcher (1579–1625), John Ford (1586–1639), John Day (1574-1640), John Marston (1576-1634), John Webster (1580-1634), Nathan Field (1587-1620), Philip Massinger (1584-1640), Richard Burbage (1567-1619), Robert Greene (1558-1592), Thomas Dekker (1575-1625), Thomas Kyd (1558-1594), William Haughton (died 1605), William Rowley (1585-1626).

It's a daunting list and confirms that to top that made you a very special talent indeed.

Thomas Middleton – A Concise Bibliography

It has long been recognised that the modern concept of authorship was rather more elastic in centuries past. Writers were not only for hire, and their work therefore a commodity, but their plays ran much shorter lengths; two weeks being a common term of performance. To that themes and scenes were liberally excised from one play and used in another. Revisions to past plays that were being restaged would be undertaken and entirely credited to other writers. Many works and plays were unpublished and have not survived and some only from memory by actors etc. Whilst many of these playwrights are only now feted for their talents, some undoubtedly were at the time, but it is difficult to, in every case, to establish exact provenance. With modern scholarly and literary techniques author attributions have sometimes changed or been re-balanced. For those where this may be the case we have placed the *Play's Title and other information* in italics

Plays
Blurt, Master Constable or The Spaniard's Night Walk (with Thomas Dekker (1602)
The Phoenix (1603–4)

The Honest Whore, Part 1, a city comedy (1604), (with Thomas Dekker)
Michaelmas Term, a city comedy, (1604)
All's Well That Ends Well (1604-5); believed by some to be co-written by Middleton based on stylometric analysis.
A Trick to Catch the Old One, a city comedy (1605)
A Mad World, My Masters, a city comedy (1605)
A Yorkshire Tragedy, a one-act tragedy (1605); attributed to Shakespeare on its title page, but stylistic analysis favours Middleton.
Timon of Athens a tragedy (1605–6); stylistic analysis indicates that Middleton may have written this play in collaboration with William Shakespeare.
The Puritan (1606)
The Revenger's Tragedy (1606). Earlier editions often mistakenly attribute authorship to Cyril Tourneur.
Your Five Gallants, a city comedy (1607)
The Family of Love (1607) some attribute this to Middleton others include Dekker and Lording Barry.
The Bloody Banquet (1608–9); co-written with Thomas Dekker.
The Roaring Girl, a city comedy depicting the exploits of Mary Frith (1611); with Thomas Dekker.
No Wit, No Help Like a Woman's, a tragic-comedy (1611)
The Second Maiden's Tragedy, a tragedy (1611); an anonymous manuscript; stylistic analysis indicates Middleton's authorship (though one scholar also attributed it to Shakespeare.
A Chaste Maid in Cheapside, a city comedy (1613)
Wit at Several Weapons, a city comedy (1613); printed as part of the Beaumont and Fletcher Folio, but stylistic analysis indicates comprehensive revision by Middleton & Rowley.
More Dissemblers Besides Women, a tragicomedy (1614)
The Widow (1615–16)
The Witch, a tragicomedy (1616)
A Fair Quarrel, a tragicomedy (1616). Co-written with William Rowley.
The Old Law, a tragicomedy (1618–19). written with William Rowley and perhaps a third collaborator.
Hengist, King of Kent, or The Mayor of Quinborough, a tragedy (1620)
Women Beware Women, a tragedy (1621)
Measure for Measure (1603-4); some scholars argue that the First Folio text was partly revised by Middleton in 1621.
Anything for a Quiet Life, a city comedy (1621). Co-written with John Webster.
The Changeling, a tragedy (1622). Co-written with William Rowley.
The Nice Valour (1622). Printed as part of the Beaumont and Fletcher Folio, but stylistic analysis indicates comprehensive revision by Middleton.
The Spanish Gypsy, a tragicomedy (1623). Believed to be a play by Middleton & Rowley and later revised by Thomas Dekker and John Ford.
A Game at Chess, a political satire (1624). Satirized the negotiations over the proposed marriage of Prince Charles, son of James I of England, with the Spanish princess. Closed after nine performances.

Masques & Entertainments
The Whole Royal and Magnificent Entertainment Given to King James Through the City of London (1603–4). Co-written with Thomas Dekker, Stephen Harrison & Ben Jonson.
The Manner of his Lordship's Entertainment
The Triumphs of Truth
Civitas Amor
The Triumphs of Honour and Industry (1617)

The Masque of Heroes, or, The Inner Temple Masque (1619)
The Triumphs of Love and Antiquity (1619)
The World Tossed at Tennis (1620). Co-written with William Rowley.
Honourable Entertainments (1620–1)
An Invention (1622)
The Sun in Aries (1621)
The Triumphs of Honour and Virtue (1622)
The Triumphs of Integrity with The Triumphs of the Golden Fleece (1623)
The Triumphs of Health and Prosperity (1626)

Poetry
The Wisdom of Solomon Paraphrased (1597)
Microcynicon: Six Snarling Satires (1599)
The Ghost of Lucrece (1600)
Burbage epitaph (1619)
Bolles epitaph (1621)
Duchess of Malfi (commendatory poem) (1623)
St James (1623)
To the King (1624)

Prose
The Penniless Parliament of Threadbare Poets (1601)
News from Gravesend. Co-written with Thomas Dekker (1603)
The Nightingale and the Ant aka Father Hubbard's Tales (1604)
The Meeting of Gallants at an Ordinary (1604). Co-written with Thomas Dekker.
Plato's Cap Cast at the Year 1604 (1604)
The Black Book (1604)
Sir Robert Sherley his Entertainment in Cracovia (1609) (translation).
The Two Gates of Salvation (1609), or The Marriage of the Old and New Testament.
The Owl's Almanac (1618)
The Peacemaker (1618)

John Fletcher – A Short Biography

John Fletcher was born in December, 1579 in Rye, Sussex. He was baptised on December 20th.

As can be imagined details of much of his life and career have not survived and, accordingly, only a very brief indication of his life and works can be given.

His father, Richard Fletcher, was a successful and rather ambitious cleric. From being the Dean of Peterborough he moved on to become the Bishop of Bristol, Bishop of Worcester and finally, shortly before his death, the Bishop of London. He was also the chaplain to Queen Elizabeth.

When he was Dean of Peterborough, Richard Fletcher, witnessed the execution of Mary, Queen of Scots. It was said he "knelt down on the scaffold steps and started to pray out loud and at length, in a prolonged and rhetorical style, as though determined to force his way into the pages of history". He cried out at her death, "So perish all the Queen's enemies!" All very dramatic but the family did have strong links to the Arts.

Young Fletcher appears at the very young age of eleven to have entered Corpus Christi College at Cambridge University in 1591. There are no records that he ever took a degree but there is some small evidence that he was being prepared for a career in the church.

However what is clear is that this was soon abandoned as he joined the stream of people who would leave University and decamp to the more bohemian life of commercial theatre in London.

Unfortunately his father fell out with Queen Elizabeth but appears to have been on his way to rehabilitation before his death in 1596. At his death he was, however, mired in debt.

The upbringing of the now teenage Fletcher and his seven siblings now passed to his paternal uncle, the poet and minor official Giles Fletcher. Giles, who had the patronage of the Earl of Essex may have been a liability rather than an advantage to the young Fletcher. With Essex involved in the failed rebellion against Elizabeth Giles was also tainted by association.

By 1606 John Fletcher appears to have equipped himself with the talents to become a playwright. Initially this appears to have been for the Children of the Queen's Revels, then performing at the Blackfriars Theatre.

Commendatory verses by Richard Brome in the Beaumont and Fletcher 1647 folio place Fletcher in the company of Ben Jonson, although it is not known when this friendship began. Jonson, of course, was a leviathan of English Literature, so admired that many of his literary friends and colleagues were simply known as 'Sons of Ben'. Fletcher's frequent early collaborator, Francis Beaumont, was also a friend of Jonson's.

Fletcher's early career was marked by one significant failure; The Faithful Shepherdess, his adaptation of Giovanni Battista Guarini's Il Pastor Fido, which was performed by the Blackfriars Children in 1608. In the preface to the printed edition of his play, Fletcher explained the failure as due to his audience's faulty expectations. They expected a pastoral tragicomedy to feature dances, comedy, and murder, with the shepherds presented in conventional stereotypes – as Fletcher put it, wearing "gray cloaks, with curtailed dogs in strings." Fletcher's preface is however best known for its pithy definition of tragicomedy: "A tragicomedy is not so called in respect of mirth and killing, but in respect it wants [i.e., lacks] deaths, which is enough to make it no tragedy; yet brings some near it, which is enough to make it no comedy." A comedy, he went on to say, must be "a representation of familiar people." His preface is critical of drama that features characters whose action violates nature.

In that case, Fletcher appears to have been developing a new style faster than audiences could comprehend. By 1609, however, he had found his stride. With Beaumont, he wrote Philaster, which became a hit for the King's Men and began a profitable association between Fletcher and that company. Philaster appears also to have begun a trend for tragicomedy. Fletcher's influence has also been said to have inspired some features of Shakespeare's late romances, and certainly his influence on the tragicomic work of other playwrights is even more marked.

By the middle of the 1610s, Fletcher's plays had achieved a popularity that rivalled Shakespeare's and cemented the pre-eminence of the King's Men in Jacobean London. After Beaumont's retirement, necessitated by ill-health, and then his early death in 1616, Fletcher continued working, both singly and in collaboration, until his death in 1625. By that time, he had produced, or had been credited with, close to fifty plays. This body of work remained a major part of the King's Men's repertory until the closing of the theatres in 1642 due to the Civil War.

At the beginning of his career Fletcher's most important collaborator was Francis Beaumont. The two wrote together for close to a decade, first for the Children of the Queen's Revels, and then for the King's Men. According to an anecdote transmitted or invented by John Aubrey, they also lived together in Bankside, sharing clothes and having "one wench in the house between them." This domestic arrangement, if it existed, was ended by Beaumont's marriage in 1613, and their dramatic partnership ended after Beaumont fell ill, probably of a stroke, that same year.

At this point Fletcher had written many plays with Beaumont and several others on his own. He seems to have been regarded as quite a talent although it should be remembered that playwrights were required to be prolific, to easily work with other collaborators and to produce work of quality and commercial appeal very quickly.

The King's Men, run by Philip Henslowe, was the most prestigious of the theatre companies and Fletcher now had an increasingly close association with it.

Fletcher collaborated with Shakespeare on Henry VIII, The Two Noble Kinsmen, and the now lost Cardenio, which some scholars say was the basis for Lewis Theobald's play Double Falsehood. (Theobald is regarded as one of the best Shakespearean editors. Whether his play is based on Cardenio or on some other is not absolutely known although Theobald certainly promoted it as his revision of the lost Shakespeare/Fletcher play.)

A play that Fletcher also wrote by himself at this time, The Woman's Prize or the Tamer Tamed, is also regarded as a sequel to The Taming of the Shrew.

In 1616, with the death of Shakespeare, Fletcher now appears to have entered into an enhanced arrangement with the King's Men on very similar terms to Shakespeare's. Fletcher would now write exclusively for the King's Men until his own death almost a decade later.

As well as continuing his solo productions Fletcher was still collaborating with other playwrights, mainly Philip Massinger, who, in turn, would succeed him as the in-house playwright for the King's Men.

Fletcher's popularity continued throughout his life; indeed during the winter of 1621, he had three of his plays performed at court. His mastery is most notable in two dramatic types; tragicomedy and the comedy of manners.

John Fletcher died in 1625, it is thought of bubonic plague which, at the time, was undergoing further outbreaks.

He seems to have been buried in what is now Southwark Cathedral, although a precise location is not known. There is much made of an anecdote that Fletcher and Massinger (who died in 1640) share the same grave but it is more likely that both are buried within a few yards of each other and that the stone markers in the floor have confused the issue. One is marked 'Edmond Shakespeare 1607' and the other 'John Fletcher 1625' refers to Shakespeare's younger brother and the playwright. The churchyards were, more often than not, completely over-crowded and breeding grounds for disease. Precise record keeping was not a practiced skill.

During the later Commonwealth, many of the playwright's best-known scenes were kept alive as drolls. These were brief performances, usually condensed into one or two scenes and with the addition of music or song to satisfy the taste for plays while the theatres were closed under the Puritians. At the re-opening of the theatres in 1660, the plays in the Fletcher canon, in original form or revised, were by far the most common productions on the English stage. The most frequently revived plays suggest the developing taste for comedies of manners. Among the tragedies, The Maid's Tragedy and, especially, Rollo Duke of Normandy held the stage. Four tragicomedies (A King and No King, The Humorous Lieutenant, Philaster, and The Island Princess) were popular, perhaps in part for their similarity to and foreshadowing of heroic drama. Four comedies (Rule a Wife And Have a Wife, The Chances, Beggars' Bush, and especially The Scornful Lady) were also stage mainstays.

Despite his popularity, and it appears he was held in higher regard than Shakespeare at this time, his works steadily lost ground to those of Shakespeare and to new productions from other playwrights.

Since then Fletcher has increasingly become a subject only for occasional revivals and for specialists. Fletcher and his collaborators have been the subject of important bibliographic and critical studies, but the plays have been revived only infrequently.

Due to the frequent collaborations between all manner of playwrights, and the revisions carried out in later years, having a settled list of authorship to any given set of plays can be problematic. The works of Fletcher and others of this period most definitely fall into this category. It is as well to take into account that during this period theatres were quite often closed either due to outbreaks of the plague or to the prevailing political and moral climate. Printers, anxious to provide materials that would sell, were not above changing a name or two to enhance sales.

Although Fletcher collaborated most often with Beaumont and Massinger, it is believed that Massinger revised many of the plays some time after their original production. Other collaborators including Nathan Field, William Shakespeare, William Rowley and others also can be seen distinctly in Fletchers' works. Many modern scholars point out that Fletcher had many particular mannerisms but other playwrights would also duplicate these at times so allocating exact contributions of anyone to a play is somewhat of a detective case in many instances. However from the original folio printings or licensing via the Master of the Revels (the statutory licensing authority to approve and censor plays as well a hand in publication and printing of theatrical materials) as well as contemporary notes a fairly precise bibliography of the works can be given with only a few plays lacking substantial authority and provenance.

John Fletcher – A Concise Bibliography

This bibliography gives the most likely date of writing together with when published, revised or licensed by the Master or the Revels (This position within the royal household was originally for royal festivities, ie revels, and later to oversee stage censorship, until this function was transferred to the Lord Chamberlain in 1624).

Solo Plays
The Faithful Shepherdess, pastoral (written 1608–9; printed 1609)
The Tragedy of Valentinian, tragedy (1610–14; 1647)
Monsieur Thomas, comedy (c. 1610–16; 1639)
The Woman's Prize, or The Tamer Tamed, comedy (c. 1611; 1647)
Bonduca, tragedy (1611–14; 1647)
The Chances, comedy (c. 1613–25; 1647)
Wit Without Money, comedy (c. 1614; 1639)
The Mad Lover, tragicomedy (acted 5 January 1617; 1647)
The Loyal Subject, tragicomedy (licensed 16 November 1618; revised 1633; 1647)
The Humorous Lieutenant, tragicomedy (c. 1619; 1647)
Women Pleased, tragicomedy (c. 1619–23; 1647)
The Island Princess, tragicomedy (c. 1620; 1647)
The Wild Goose Chase, comedy (c. 1621; 1652)
The Pilgrim, comedy (c. 1621; 1647)
A Wife for a Month, tragicomedy (licensed 27 May 1624; 1647)
Rule a Wife and Have a Wife, comedy (licensed 19 October 1624; 1640)

Collaborations

With Francis Beaumont
The Woman Hater, comedy (1606; 1607)
Cupid's Revenge, tragedy (c. 1607–12; 1615)
Philaster, or Love Lies a-Bleeding, tragicomedy (c. 1609; 1620)
The Maid's Tragedy, Tragedy (c. 1609; 1619)
A King and No King, tragicomedy (1611; 1619)
The Captain, comedy (c. 1609–12; 1647)
The Scornful Lady, comedy (c. 1613; 1616)
Love's Pilgrimage, tragicomedy (c. 1615–16; 1647)
The Noble Gentleman, comedy (c. 1613; licensed 3 February 1626; 1647)

With Francis Beaumont & Philip Massinger
Thierry & Theodoret, tragedy (c. 1607; 1621)
The Coxcomb, comedy (c. 1608–10; 1647)
Beggars' Bush, comedy (c. 1612–13; revised 1622; 1647)
Love's Cure, comedy (c. 1612–13; revised 1625; 1647)

With Philip Massinger
Sir John van Olden Barnavelt, tragedy (August 1619; MS)
The Little French Lawyer, comedy (c. 1619–23; 1647)
A Very Woman, tragicomedy (c. 1619–22; licensed 6 June 1634; 1655)
The Custom of the Country, comedy (c. 1619–23; 1647)
The Double Marriage, tragedy (c. 1619–23; 1647)
The False One, history (c. 1619–23; 1647)

The Prophetess, tragicomedy (licensed 14 May 1622; 1647)
The Sea Voyage, comedy (licensed 22 June 1622; 1647)
The Spanish Curate, comedy (licensed 24 October 1622; 1647)
The Lovers' Progress or The Wandering Lovers, tragicomedy (licensed 6 December 1623; rev 1634; 1647)
The Elder Brother, comedy (c. 1625; 1637)

With Philip Massinger & Nathan Field
The Honest Man's Fortune, tragicomedy (1613; 1647)
The Queen of Corinth, tragicomedy (c. 1616–18; 1647)
The Knight of Malta, tragicomedy (c. 1619; 1647)

With William Shakespeare
Henry VIII, history (c. 1613; 1623)
The Two Noble Kinsmen, tragicomedy (c. 1613; 1634)
Cardenio, tragicomedy (c. 1613)

With Thomas Middleton & William Rowley
Wit at Several Weapons, comedy (c. 1610–20; 1647)

With William Rowley
The Maid in the Mill (licensed 29 August 1623; 1647).

With Nathan Field
Four Plays, or Moral Representations, in One, morality (c. 1608–13; 1647)

With Philip Massinger, Ben Jonson and George Chapman
Rollo Duke of Normandy, or The Bloody Brother, tragedy (c. 1617; revised 1627–30; 1639)

With James Shirley
The Night Walker, or The Little Thief, comedy (c. 1611; 1640)
The Coronation c. 1635

Uncertain
The Nice Valour, or The Passionate Madman, comedy (c. 1615–25; 1647)
The Laws of Candy, tragicomedy (c. 1619–23; 1647)
The Fair Maid of the Inn, comedy (licensed 22 January 1626; 1647)
The Faithful Friends, tragicomedy (registered 29 June 1660; MS.)

The Nice Valour is possibly by Fletcher revised by Thomas Middleton;

The Fair Maid of the Inn is perhaps a play by Massinger, John Ford, and John Webster, either with or without Fletcher's involvement.

The Laws of Candy has been variously attributed to Fletcher and to John Ford.

The Night-Walker was a Fletcher original, with additions by Shirley for a 1639 production.

Even now there is not absolute certainty on several of the plays. The first Beaumont & Fletcher folio of 1647 contained 35 plays and the second folio of 1679 added a further 18. In total 53 plays.

The first folio included The Masque of the Inner Temple and Gray's Inn (1613), and the second The Knight of the Burning Pestle (1607), widely considered Beaumont's solo works, although the latter was in early editions attributed to both writers. Fletcher himself said that Beaumont was attributed so-authorship of many works that belonged solely to Fletcher or to other collaborators.

One play in the canon, Sir John Van Olden Barnavelt, existed in manuscript and was not published till 1883.